Living Your
PURPOSE

The Heart of NLP

by Linda R. Ferguson, Ph.D.

Copyright © 2014 by Linda R. Ferguson
First Edition – June 2014

ISBN
978-1-4602-1455-8 (Hardcover)
978-1-4602-1456-5 (Paperback)
978-1-4602-1457-2 (eBook)

All rights reserved.

No part of this publication may be reproduced in any form, or by any means, electronic or mechanical, including photocopying, recording, or any information browsing, storage, or retrieval system, without permission in writing from the publisher.

Produced by:

FriesenPress
Suite 300 – 852 Fort Street
Victoria, BC, Canada V8W 1H8

www.friesenpress.com

Distributed to the trade by The Ingram Book Company

Table of Contents

What Do You Want? 1
    The heart of NLP   4
    The language of NLP   8
    Four reasons to explore NLP   10
    Living your purpose takes practice   15
    How to read this book   16

Mind/Body Integration 19
    Mind/body integration and managing pain   21
    Solving problems through mind/body integration   27
    Mind/body connections open up new possibilities   32
    Setting goals through mind/body integration   35

People Have What They Need 41
    Getting to the resources beyond the pain   42
    Knowing you have the next piece of the puzzle   47
    Win by bringing out the best in other people   52
    Know what you really want   56

TABLE OF CONTENTS CONTINUED...

Moving on Common Ground 65
    Is a chronic illness a frenemy?   67
    Discovering common ground when solving a problem   71
    All influence springs from common ground   77
    Set yourself up for success   82

Patterns Work Like Magic 89
    Make the pattern bigger than the pain   91
    Walk away from the problem you want to solve   97
    Pattern recognition is the key to influence   101
    Find the pattern around your next big decision   106

Living on Purpose 113
    Is healing a default or a choice?   115
    Who does the healing?   116
    Does purpose trump problem?   121
    Let purpose drive your process   123
    Having a purpose is a giant step towards influence   126
    Do you need a purpose to set a goal?   131

The PATH to Change that Satisfies 137
    The PATH for making things happen   139
    Next steps in NLP   142
    And as we end, my thanks for help along the way   144

References 147

What Do You Want?

NLP (neurolinguistic programming) has been defined in many ways. One easy way to understand it is that it is a path that many people have taken to move towards increased satisfaction and achievement. This path isn't made of dirt or asphalt. NLP is made of techniques for changing perceptions as you explore new territory to move towards your destination. Like other paths, it offers proof with every step that you are not the first person to walk this way and that the steps of the people before you can make your own progress easier and more secure.

The first step on this path is the one that separates the good from the bad in NLP and other models of change. How do you choose your destination? People who begin with the belief that knowing what they want is easy will often start off in the wrong direction. They begin chasing the first goals that come to mind or the goals that other people set for them. These top-of-mind goals are often a wish list, sometimes filtered to be a wish list of things that are possible and within their control. Initially there is a rush of excitement and a new focus on self-esteem as they make things happen. Later there is the messiness of discovering that they do not entirely like what they wanted. You know the phrase "be careful what you wish for." It's a useful caution in a world where psychologists believe we are mostly terrible at predicting our emotions (Gilbert, *The Surprising Science of Happiness*). It's easy to want things but it is much harder to want things that will contribute to a life well-lived. We should be asking: what do you want that will nurture and satisfy the person you are now and the person you will be in the future?

The answer begins with curiosity about what already has value in your life and experience. We are better at remembering what is meaningful to us than we are at constructing an imagined future and knowing that we will value it. Much of NLP is concerned with finding the way forward by paying attention to what has already worked or what is already of value. Although it may be hard to articulate a comprehensive purpose that ties together the experiences you value, it is possible to pay attention to what you value and assume it has value because it is aligned with a purpose. Purpose is the one big goal that allows us to know whether we are stepping off the path or moving in the right direction.

As a path, NLP defines a process for making change happen by knowing what you want, taking action, testing the results you get, and doing more of what works. It's not magic. At the heart of NLP is a set of concepts and processes that have been validated through research in fields from psychology to business to behavioural economics. These processes can produce magical results. Sometimes, people accuse NLP of the kind of magic that is all illusion. This happens when people have not done the work to uncover the goals that will satisfy them. Those people pursue a vision of what they think they want and hold it in their hands for just a moment before finding they do not really want it. At other times, NLP feels magical because everything simply clicks into place. When you are open to the self that includes all your memories and unconscious processes, you sometimes discover that you are smarter, happier and more capable than you thought you were. Knowing for sure that you are moving on solid ground, you can make more progress than you thought possible. The process of achieving what you want works so smoothly with your natural strengths that the results can seem like the best kind of magic.

In this book, I will introduce one more aspect of the magic of NLP. I'm going to pull back the curtain on five principles (in NLP they are called presuppositions) that will help you find and get what you really want. These principles are beliefs, not facts. At any given moment in any given situation, they may or may not be true. The key value in NLP is not truth, but usefulness. If you are not sure how something untrue could be useful, I will give you two examples. The first is the growing evidence that some amount of optimism allows people to achieve better results than realism. Although realism is closer to the truth, optimism is a characteristic that seems to breed success in entrepreneurs and resilience in everyone (Bannink, p. 53). The second example I will offer is the usefulness of fiction (whether it comes in the form of movies, books, comics or video games). All fictions offer us something that is labelled "untrue" so that we can imagine an experience that is different than our current reality.

Within the frame of NLP, these principles were derived from the work of brilliant therapists and other models of excellence who were able to direct change in other people. Outside the frame of NLP, these same concepts are important in many models related to positive psychology. Optimism and fictions are both examples of how it can be useful to suspend disbelief long enough to generate new insights. So are these five principles. If you think and act as if these principles were true, you will naturally change, communicate and achieve as though you were using NLP. Acting as if they are true will lead to new insights and allow you to take new steps on the path to what you want.

The heart of NLP

Descriptions of what NLP is and how it works tend to be confusing. Paradoxically, they are confusing because NLP works in ways that are so much a part of human experience that we often forget to think about them at all. What do a surgeon, a software sales representative and an Olympic athlete have in common? They could all use the same processes to maintain high performance states, learn more from models of excellence, and be more aware of how and when to use instinct as part of their decision making. Those processes are the practices of NLP.

NLP is the study of how people make change on purpose. All human beings are changing all the time and all human beings are influenced by, and have influence on, the people around them. Training in change and influence does not create influence any more than training in horsemanship creates a horse. Training does create the possibility for influence that is directed towards a purpose. NLP training captures the power of natural influence and interaction for predictable, replicable results. If you've ever done something brilliant and then wished you knew how to do it again, you were wishing that you had the tools offered by NLP.

The five principles at the heart of NLP will allow you to use the tools of NLP to make change on purpose. If you do not work within the principles, you might still use the tools to get results. These results are unlikely to be either satisfying or sustaining. You are always changing so making change happen is not hard. You are always influencing other people and being influenced by them, so developing influence is not hard. Predicting the results of the change you make and the influence you develop is hard. The five principles make it more likely that your predictions will be accurate more often. They support all the NLP practices in the same way your physical heart supports your body and your emotional heart supports your sense of who you are and where you belong.

In this book, we will be focusing on one principle at a time so that you can improve your ability to notice that principle at work in your life and to use it more effectively to make the changes you want to make. At the end, we will explore how these principles support an NLP-based strategy for making change. But first, we'll focus our attention on just one principle at a time and relate it to each of the four main reasons people practice NLP. You will be able to apply the principles yourself to make changes even before you study the techniques of NLP.

These five core principles are:

1. People are integrated. The conscious mind, unconscious processes and the body are one continuous system. Changing one changes the others too.

2. People are resourceful. All people have within them the strengths and capabilities they need to live more satisfying lives.

3. People are connected. We are continually fine-tuning internal connections between mind, body and unconscious processes. In the same way, we are continually developing, directing and refining the connections between us and other people.

4. People are predictable. People work in patterns that include thought, perception and behaviours. Patterns allow us to predict the responses of other people and to do what they do and produce similar results.

5. People are purposeful. Knowing what you want leads to more satisfaction than going with the flow.

The first principle is that people are integrated: each person is one unified identity that includes mind, body and unconscious processes. That wouldn't seem remarkable except that in Western thought there has been a long, systematic separation of mind and body. We do admit that physical pain can sometimes make it hard to think clearly and research is beginning to explore the harm that emotional difficulty can do to our bodies. But generally, we set up our schools and workplaces as though all the important stuff is in people's heads and their bodies are not relevant and rather inconvenient. In his TED talk, Ken Robinson singles out academics as people who believe that their bodies exist to carry their minds around (*Ken Robinson says schools kill creativity*). This is a little unfair. The same holds true of almost all knowledge workers. Memories of the integration of mind and body linger in our language for instinct. We occasionally admit that we have replaced analysis with a "feeling" or that we can know things "in our gut." In NLP, we assume that our minds and bodies are one continuous system interacting with the world and that knowing and acting both involve the entire system.

The second core principle is that everyone has what they need to lead a more satisfying life. It is one of the principles based on "doing what works" instead of doing what we can prove is true. It's possible that not everyone does have the resources of mind, body and experience to lead a more satisfying life. But it is more useful to assume that everyone has resources that they could apply to a given situation to be happier. This is especially true when the person in question is yourself. If you assume that somewhere in you there is the wisdom, the creativity, the strength or the charisma to do what you want to do, then you become much more likely to be able to find that quality in yourself and put it to good use.

The third principle is that human beings require connection to other people and to a context. We influence people only when we are connected and we are influenced by people when we see that they have something in common with us. The ground we share might be a shared state or motivation. It might be that we are moving together towards a shared representation of a future that hasn't happened yet. Or it might be that we are moving away from shared events or a shared past. All of the movement starts when we notice our intention to move and the other people who share our starting point. We also look for common ground between what we know of our unconscious selves, our minds and our bodies. When we work with the alignment of all systems, we are more effective and more satisfied.

The fourth of the five core principles is that people understand a complex reality through patterns. No information exists outside of its context and no information is stored by the human brain unless it is stored as part of a cognitive web. Individual pieces of information have no meaning in and of themselves. Meaning is found in the patterns that contain and shape the data. NLP provides training in how to work with the relationships among data rather than with data points individually. Wherever NLP has been tempted to focus on individual data points (like eye movements), it has failed to offer convincing evidence that it works. Wherever NLP has focused on patterning (in language and in body language), it has been effective in allowing practitioners to grab more accurate meaning more quickly. It is natural to get caught up in the details. It is genius to be able to see the trends (which are patterns) and influence them as they develop.

The final principle is the one that determines how we build meaning and value into our lives. People with a sense of purpose are better off than people who do not know what they want. A purpose allows us to set goals. Goals detach us from the present and tempt us to manipulate what we perceive now so that we will like something we may or may not achieve in the future. By separating us from an immersion in the present, goals offer us both freedom and meaning, landmarks and benchmarks so that we can know that we are making progress towards something that matters to us. Our brains feature complicated processes for filtering the impossibly complex information that the world presents to us each day. Some of those processes look for a fit between what is around us and what we want. Purpose allows us to live in a world where it is possible to find what we need to have what we want.

What are the implications of reminding oneself over and over of these five core principles? First you will solve the application problems that attracted you to NLP. Next you will find that you are changing to become fundamentally more positive in focus, more optimistic in outlook, and more creative in shaping useful collaborations with more different people.

The language of NLP

In this book, I have explained the effectiveness of NLP in terms that are in wide use inside and outside NLP. There are a few terms that are used in NLP in ways that might be unfamiliar to you. I have used them because their use in NLP is consistent with their use outside NLP and because I think they meet the standards of the best language everywhere. They are an elegant way to represent a useful concept.

1. State. In NLP, the word "state" represents a person's total experience at a given moment in time. State includes sensory awareness, physiology, thoughts and emotions. Different states support different behaviours and peak performance is achieved by matching the right state to a task.

2. Resource. In NLP, a resource is any experience, thought, quality or behaviour that will help you move through life in a more satisfying way. Often these resources need to be retrieved through conscious thought and applied intentionally to the circumstances or situations that need to be improved so that you can move forward.

3. Congruence. In NLP, congruence describes a state of being where your thoughts, memories, emotions, sensory perceptions and physiology all seem to be engaged in doing just one thing. When congruence supports peak performance, it is related to that state of energized, relaxed focus that has been called "flow" (Csikszentmihalyi) or being in the zone. In NLP, recognizing congruence allows you to notice when your conscious mind is aligned with your unconscious processes.

4. Incongruence, on the other hand, is a sign that you are managing multiple streams of information for more than one task. This is not always a bad thing. Your unconscious processes are always monitoring your physical well-being, even when your mind seems wholly occupied in just one thing. Parents rely on multi-tasking to do household tasks while monitoring the safety of their children. Most work involves monitoring an environment while focusing on one's own tasks. Incongruence is never as strong as congruence but it can be useful and comfortable.

5. Pattern. Although pattern is a term widely used to describe elements or behaviours that recur in the same relationship to produce the same results, it is not widely used in everyday speech. Patterns are hard to describe in words because they involve many simultaneous relationships and language is linear and can only describe one relationship at a time. If it seems unfamiliar, you will soon notice that this word means exactly what you expect it to mean.

6. Calibration. To calibrate is to notice difference in relation to a standard measurement or benchmark. In NLP, calibration is a process that allows you to pay attention to particular states in people and then recognize those states when they occur again.

Like any path that moves over lots of territory, NLP has offshoots that promised a better route but proved less useful than the main path. Many of these are marked by complicated jargon and processes that are not consistent with current research in neuroscience and behavioural science. They seem to work for some people, but for most people they are not the best way to move in the desired direction. We know more about how the brain works now than we did when NLP was first developed and many of the processes and techniques of NLP have also been developed in other fields where they may be known by different names.

If you were first introduced to NLP through eye patterns, the meta model or meta programs, you may be surprised that they are not mentioned in this book. As useful as those have been to some people, they are often not consistent with the main stream of science and they are not necessary to get productive results using the processes that are consistent with current best practice in human thought and change management. In the interests of understanding and practical application, I have avoided any techniques that require more specialized jargon.

I have a doctorate in English Literature and my own beliefs about language come from the poets who shaped my thought. Like them, I believe in using the simplest words that will carry my meaning. I have worked to do so throughout this book.

Four reasons to explore NLP

Equipped with an understanding of the five core principles, we are ready to approach the challenges which most often motivate people to explore NLP. From a certain point of view, the only problem that human beings face is how to identify and maintain states, activities and goals that make them feel congruent. Congruence is a sign that our minds, bodies and unconscious processes are in alignment. This alignment is our signal that we are living our purpose. We are acting to create the relationship between ourselves, other people and the environment that is the big goal that sets the direction for our path. From this perspective, all motivation is a motivation to resolve dissonance so that we can be aware of the congruence that signals we are living our purpose.

There are four obstacles that make it difficult to maintain a sense of congruence. The first is pain. The experience of pain breaks the connections between unconscious processes, the body and the mind. When in pain, we lose awareness that the pain is temporary and partial and that we have access to a rich storehouse of other resources and intentions. Whether pain causes the separation of the self into fragments or is a sign that the fragmentation has occurred is not as important as managing the pain to restore congruence and movement in alignment with your purpose. When pain is resolved, we can move to dealing with the problem that caused the pain. The desire to solve problems is the second motivation for studying and applying NLP techniques. The third motivation is the desire to connect more effectively with other people. The human brain monitors other human beings through a series of automatic reactions that occur without our willing them and that will either pull us into congruence or pull us in different directions. People study NLP so that they can be more aware of the influence they exert on others and the influence that is affecting their own states and actions. Finally, people come to NLP as a way to set goals for themselves. Deciding what you want often means enduring some incongruence as you separate out the influence of other people, pain and problems and identify the next step on the path set by your purpose.

1. Pain management

The most basic incongruence occurs when the mind and the body pull in different directions. This is experienced as tension, distress and pain. Sometimes the pain has a physical cause and sometimes it is caused by emotions, but both are felt in the body. We know our emotions by the impact they have on our physiologies, and we experience pain in our bodies even when the source is not physical. Pain is often described as the basic "away from" motivation. In this model we seek healing so that the pain will stop. But that doesn't explain why so many people are willing to endure pain if it helps them reach a goal. A better way of looking at pain is to see it as a division in which the body and the mind want different things. The resolution of pain is the ability to focus so completely on a goal that the pain is either not present or can be tolerated. This is as true of a small business facing growing pain as it is of an individual who needs to resolve past trauma before moving ahead. The antidote for pain is not comfort. It is a frame in which the pain is contained by a congruent purpose.

2. Problem solving

We experience another form of uncomfortable incongruence when we face a problem or a puzzle for which there is no apparent answer. The most basic motivation for learning is the desire for new skills or information to apply to problems which have so far resisted our efforts to solve them. People often turn to NLP for "outside the box" thinking and heightened powers of observation. They are looking for accelerated techniques for encountering, absorbing, and using new information to solve existing problems. A problem creates congruence when it represents a stretch. It must be solvable with effort. Problems that cannot be solved by stretching create incongruence, as part of the mind splits off to work on what is

ClaimSecure eProfile
user: MikG4   password: wmR666aK

1. Book to library
2. to book appt with Dr. Burman
3. To buy diper cream
4. to fill an OHIP application for Maria

Amazon-
10 Concordia.

Leas@jiastoronto.org

"Haste Naboshi" = working hard

possible while another part works away at the whole problem. Problems are transformed when they stop taking up the whole of your awareness and become one step towards the information you need to develop or embody a purpose. As you acquire more information, you are no longer stopped by the problem you have not yet solved.

3. *Effective connections with other people*

The third kind of incongruence that people work to resolve through NLP is the kind of conflict that happens between people. It's important to recall here that we all carry a whole community of people in our heads. We are all born to be accurate, interested observers of the people around us, and we store the patterns we observe in our own neurology to be used or changed as necessary. Our internal congruence often depends on being able to resolve differences with the versions of other people who live inside our thoughts. Externally, we also seek congruence with other people. We want to get along with the people around us and to predict their behaviours and responses. When they are hard to predict, we often get caught up in conflict. We pull in one direction while they pull in another until something — or someone — snaps.

People who have particularly strong influence are often able to draw other people into congruence with their beliefs or behaviours. They remain internally congruent because they are able to predict other people's behaviour (and not be distracted by it). In fact, some of the most powerful influencers are sociopaths who are able to influence precisely because they can manipulate other people's reality without paying the price of becoming incongruent (Dutton, 2011). For most people, the price of manipulating other people is a cycle of self-doubt and incongruence. What we all need, it seems, are techniques for influencing other people that are respectful of our human connections and of our unconscious drives to connect and to be connected with others.

NLP provides a terrific set of practices to create common ground so that you can be both congruent and influential. People study NLP to understand how to manage the boundaries between themselves and others so that they can have influence without sacrificing their beliefs about themselves and their world. They become better at discovering genuinely common ground and building on that common ground so that their agreements are sustainable and effective. Leaders learn to respect and work with their own congruence and the congruence of their team members so that influence is a positive force for engaging and directing.

4. Defining goals and setting your direction

Leaders use their influence to move themselves and others towards the accomplishment of a goal or purpose. NLP has been famed (and sometimes defamed) as a way to set and achieve goals by changing perception and manipulating connection. A goal can either focus the mind or create distracting tension. Good goals are those that are congruent with a larger purpose. Research suggests that it is optimal to have goals that can be reached only by stretching (Bannink, p. 86). Imagine reaching for an apple on a branch that is just slightly out of reach. If it were lower, you would pick it and move on. If it were higher, it would be too high, and you would walk away. But if the apple is just out of reach, you will forget everything as you imagine various ways of bringing the apple just a little closer. Even as you read these words, you are almost aware of your field of vision closing around that apple, and the stretch of your body as you strain towards it. NLP provides techniques for stretching farther and techniques for building the resilience to continue reaching even after you have failed once or twice.

LIVING YOUR **PURPOSE**

LIVING YOUR PURPOSE TAKES PRACTICE

In summary, then, people look for ways to gain or maintain congruence in the face of a world where needs and circumstances are always changing. People are thrown into incongruence by pain, problems, other people and the wrong goals. NLP offers five beliefs that enable people to move past their incongruence and develop a personal sense of purpose. These beliefs frame responses to situations so that individuals can be engaged, effective and congruent.

I don't know what resources you have or what strengths you might uncover under the right circumstances. Neither do you. Our hidden selves are truly hidden from our conscious awareness until something or someone reflects them back to us or pulls them into the light. We can choose to assume we have what we need to do the things that will satisfy us or we can choose to assume that we cannot be satisfied. When we choose to work hard and persist, we get stronger. Even if we do not reach the goal we had in mind, we develop strengths and we walk the path set by our purpose.

We live amid a wealth of evidence that talent and strength can be ours if we do the work, take the risks, and persist. It's not magical and it often hurts. For everyone who succeeds by chance, there are many more who succeed by practice, study and lots of work. Along the way, they discover strength, creativity, understanding and persistence they did not know they had. They discover that they have what they need to live a more satisfying life. You can discover it in the same way: uncover your purpose, set goals that serve it and do the work it takes to achieve them.

How to read this book

This book is divided into five chapters, one for each of the five beliefs at the heart of NLP. Each of the chapters is divided into four sections, one for each of the main reasons that people explore NLP. If you choose to read the whole of the book in order, you will take a journey that spirals through the process of noticing, applying and refining information about what will lead you to a life that satisfies you. You will realize that the book is coaching you through a process and you could use the same process to coach others to manage their pain, solve their problems, explore useful connections and define what they want. Embedded in the framing here is the idea that this process is a spiral. You learn something, move away to learn something else, then return to the original learning to refine, enlarge or modify it. NLP, like life, is a path with many twists and turns.

If you are impatient with twists and turns, you might choose to start reading at the belief that makes the most sense to you. Throughout the book I will be advocating for *guess and test* as an approach to new information. Guess what will be useful or true, and then apply it in your life and test its usefulness. If you are working on a particular issue, instead of reading all of one chapter, you might read the sections in each chapter that apply to that issue (read all the sections on pain, for instance). Just *guess and test* to engage with the material and discover how it is useful to you and then follow your interest to another section or chapter.

Some of you might just want to browse the book, trusting your instincts to guide you to the section that you need immediately to think differently about a decision that has you stuck. I would suggest that you read all of one section (usually an explanation, an illustration or story, an exercise and a summary) for best results. Only you know where you are on the path to your own satisfying life, and your interest will be a useful guide to what will work for you.

The book contains the stories of my interactions with clients over the past ten years. All of the examples in this book are based on a composite of several people. I will include details from two or three different people and use pseudonyms to protect their identities. It's a way of showing you what these beliefs can accomplish without violating the privacy of my students and clients.

Mind/Body Integration

Let's begin with the most easily tested of the beliefs of NLP: the human mind and body form one continuous system. Nothing happens in one without leaving an impact on the other. A threat to one is a threat to both. As a human being, you know yourself to be the person who lives inside your skin. Our bodies give us edges that define who and how we are in the world. The "you" inside the body is a mind. Our minds give meaning and edges to what we perceive in the physical world. NLP does not make value judgments about whether we should distinguish between mind and body. NLP rests on a foundation that says whether or not it should be true, we benefit when we act as though mind and body form one continuous and integrated system.

It seems obvious that our minds and our bodies connect through our brains. We assume that our thoughts and our sense of self reside in our brain and then connect with the rest of us through our neurology. Our brains have room for our thoughts, but they also provide real estate to our physical sensations. In the brain, the activity caused by thinking is about the same as the activity caused by sensory perceptions or feelings. What's more, our brains connect the mind's information with the body's information in patterns known as cognitive webs or neural webs. We can conceptualize thought as all the activity carried out in the brain at a given moment.

Neural webs are the patterns formed by the connections that the brain makes among all the neurons active at that moment. Thought no longer seems to be disembodied, separate from physical reality. Neuroscience has given us a way of understanding thought as embodied, always accompanied by sensory representations and physiological activity. When I take a bite and think "this apple is sour," the "apple" and the "sour" are both embodied thought. By this I mean that both of them represent a physical stimulus (the object or the taste) and a concept (the apple-ness of the apple, for instance). You will find, if you test this, that it is remarkably hard to have a thought that is so abstract it leaves no trace in your body or your senses. For all intents and purposes, we think with our minds and bodies at the same time.

This also leads to the idea that the conscious and unconscious minds are both active simultaneously whenever we are awake. The unconscious mind is simply the part of our mind that is not involved in language or image-making at a given moment. It is always wired into and working in concert with our conscious awareness and intention to produce expressions and behaviours. The unconscious is not so much buried or hidden as it is present in our non-verbal communications and patterns of reaction. While it is true that we lose conscious awareness of our circumstances when we sleep, it does not follow that we must lose access to unconscious processes when we are awake. Our instincts, our reflexes and our habits all work even when we are thinking consciously. This is also true of all our physiological functions. We often recognize the effects of unconscious processes by noticing changes in our sensory perceptions or physiology.

Knowing our own minds can mean knowing our bodies well enough to recognize changes in them.

Mind/body integration and managing pain

People often turn to NLP as a way of managing, getting over or getting through pain. Sometimes the pain is physical and sometimes it is emotional. They may be troubled by a trauma, a phobia or anxiety. They may have a condition that causes chronic pain or wish to accelerate their recovery from an accident or injury. In all these cases, pain has both a physical dimension and a psychological one. Physical pain limits the ability to be at one's best for mental performance. Emotional pain generally turns up in one or more places in the body. Within the practices and processes of NLP, pain is both a condition that might be healed and a communication that must be understood before the mind will agree to let go.

An NLP practitioner can coach an individual through practices that manipulate their perception of a situation. Through this coaching, the individual might be able to foster healing within their bodies or psyche. The agent of healing is always the individual himself or herself. NLP facilitates and accelerates healing processes but does not, in itself, do the healing. Does that seem like splitting hairs? They are important hairs to split because they demonstrate the difference between manipulating a process and manipulating a person. NLP practitioners should have expertise in working with processes that open up new possibilities for you. Because your mind and body are one integrated system, opening new possibilities through thought can create new opportunities for physical healing. Your intention to manage or overcome your own pain is the most important element in the way NLP works.

How does this work begin? The short version is that your whole self (mind and body, conscious and unconscious) knows more than any one part of you does. Some of what you do not know is available to people observing you. They have a perspective that allows them to see things you cannot see. The easiest example of this is to remember a time when someone asked you "What's wrong?" and you said "nothing." When you flip the situation so that you are the person doing the observing, you know that "nothing" was "something" and the evidence was in the way someone looked or moved or sounded. NLP practitioners pay attention to the words you use to explain or describe your state and to the non-verbal, often unconscious, ways you communicate clues about what is in your experience but not in your awareness. The practitioner then uses various techniques to change how you are thinking or perceiving and notices the accompanying changes in your non-verbal communication or language patterns.

The NLP practice involves observing you in a state you don't like, stimulating thoughts or movements that interrupt that state, and then eliciting the non-verbal elements of a state you like better. State here means the total of your experience at a given moment. It includes your thinking, beliefs, emotions, perceptions and physiology. If you come to a practitioner intending to heal, you will uncover a state that supports healing in you and your practitioner will help you focus on that state until you can sustain it with a combination of conscious and unconscious cues. That state will then support you in whatever healing your body or psyche needs to do.

Mind/body integration is a walk in the park

We will start with a story of healing from the deep fatigue of doing just a little too much for just a little too long. Sarah works in Human Resources for a large global corporation. She has made rapid progress and is now considering whether to establish her own company or to push harder for a promotion to Director level. Her love for her career is matched by her love for her first child, a son born eight months ago. Sarah signed up for NLP Practitioner training because she was interested in being a more effective mentor to her direct reports. But after the first day, she realized that she was experiencing more than a little burnout. She was a good wife, a good mom and a good professional and she had no idea how to maintain her performance as both her son and her work grew. She was exhausted.

What did the NLP Practitioner course offer Sarah? Yes, she learned the mechanics of how people shift their perceptions to open up new possibilities. She discovered more of what drives her and how clear she is on her goals. But the most important things she learned were not techniques. She spent time in a nearby park, learning to breathe and to walk the way people in a city park breathe and walk. As she did the exercises, she opened herself to a different pace and a rich, non-verbal experience of herself and her place in the world. At key moments, a trainer might sit with her as she breathed through her anxiety about balance and progress. At other moments, she found that she had left the anxiety on a park bench and was simply enjoying new experiences. The combined result of the NLP program was that in the months following the course she made rapid progress as a mentor and leader at work while deepening her love for her family.

An exercise to move you through pain

You probably know that there are many studies that prove that exercise and intentional breathing are both good ways to relieve or manage stress. Perhaps you have even had experiences where a great workout or a long walk cleared your head and your heart.

You can create these experiences on purpose. When you are aware that something in your life is getting in your way, when you are in pain, then you can use your breath and your body to gently move you forward. Begin by finding a place where you can walk comfortably for about fifteen minutes. You might want to choose a route that will take you in a circle, so that in fifteen minutes you will be almost back where you start. If possible, choose a place that you love, a place that is beautiful in some way. If not, the next best thing is to load an iPod with some music that makes you feel wide awake and alive. When you have everything you need, find a starting point outside.

Begin by spending a few minutes reflecting on the situation that started the problem or just noticing where and how you are experiencing some pain. Don't try to change anything yet, just be curious about what you are experiencing as you think about this pain. Then walk a few steps away from the starting point. Look back and pretend you see a version of yourself, stuck at the starting point in that situation you were imagining.

Look at the time on your phone or watch and plan to look again in about five minutes. It doesn't have to be exact, but you will find that telling yourself you will check again at a specific time makes it easier to remember to check. Once you know when you need to check the time again, set off in the direction that feels right to you. Allow yourself to move energetically enough so that you feel the blood flowing and gently enough so that you can breathe a little more deeply than usual.

After about five minutes, check the time. Notice whether you were too early or too late, but don't worry about it. Instead, take a moment and allow yourself to see a picture that represents the situation you left at the starting line. Imagine the picture about ten feet in front of you. Taking the same relaxed breaths and moving to the same soundtrack, walk up to the picture and then right through it. Use your body to tear right through the paper on which that picture was painted. Notice the paper as it falls away to either side. Look at your watch and tell yourself to stop again in about five minutes.

As you walk, you can explore the scenery. You'll find that you are curious about things along the way. You may feel playful or peaceful. Just enjoy your walk in the way that works best for you until you get a sense that five minutes must have passed. Stop and check. Notice whether your estimate was better this time, but do not let yourself get involved in judging. Judging your estimates is not the point.

Now allow yourself to hear the sounds associated with the situation that caused you pain or in which you were in pain. Imagine the sounds are coming from a place about ten feet ahead of you on the path. Walk towards the sounds, maintaining your pace and your breathing as you do. When you get to the sounds, focus on your breath and posture and move through the sounds easily. If you find you slow down, repeat the process. Hear the sounds about ten feet ahead of you on the path, and walk through them again.

Check the time. Notice what time it will be in five minutes and tell yourself that you will check again then. In the meantime, you have another five minutes to enjoy your walk. Have you been people-watching? Notice the people who really have it together, the people who are feeling great, the people who have somewhere great to go. Let some of the posture and energy you have been watching come into your own walk so that you feel energized and relaxed at the same time. Notice how your breathing changes as you adapt to this new energy.

Look ahead and pick a landmark ten or fifteen feet away. There's a spot on the sidewalk next to that garbage can or tree or whatever you have chosen. At that spot, you will walk through all the physical feelings associated with that situation. You will walk through with the same energy and posture, the same breathing and bounce. Just know they are there and walk right through them, breaking up the feelings in the same way you burst through the pictures. And now you are free.

And as you are free, you can relax and enjoy the walk back to your starting point. When you arrive there, take a moment to notice your breath. Let it be a little slower and deeper, a little more restful. Then notice how the situation you imagined you were leaving here at the beginning is different now. Begin by noticing changes in the sights and sounds. Perhaps they are farther away or smaller or lighter or less distinct. Notice changes in the physical sensation of thinking about this. Then notice that you remember exactly how your walk felt at its best, and feel that for a few moments. Finally, let yourself notice whatever else you need to notice so that you can be whole and comfortable and ready to move on.

Three steps to managing pain through mind/body integration

1. Begin by knowing that although your mind and body are one system, you and your pain are not continuous. There are already moments when you forget to be in pain. The key to being more comfortable is to notice those moments and those parts of your body or your life that are free from pain.

2. Find a place where you can move or sit comfortably. If pain prevents you from moving, sit and focus on your breath. If you can move comfortably, begin to walk. Practice noticing that your pain and you are separate. You can know the pain is there and yet breathe or move comfortably.

3. When you slip back into awareness of pain, just refocus and slip into comfortable patterns of breathing or movement.

LIVING YOUR **PURPOSE**

Solving problems through mind/body integration

Have you ever solved a tough problem by concentrating on it harder? Ironically, although we all think that "try harder" is the answer to being stuck, trying harder often just spins our wheels and we sink deeper into the rut. Most famous breakthroughs have come not from trying harder but from taking a break. Apparently we come up with the best answers by moving our attention away from a problem and letting our unconscious processes work on it in the background.

Problems often have a lot in common with catchy popular songs. They get stuck in your head and play there over and over. As much as your conscious awareness pleads for a break, you keep feeding yourself the same pattern over and over again. You might actually find that your body becomes part of the problem. You begin to associate problem solving with clenched jaws, tension in your upper body, an uncomfortable core or restless legs. The more you try to solve the problem, the more there seems to be no way out of this uncomfortable circuit. You begin to feel physically as though you were sitting in a box two sizes too small for you.

Using your body for better thinking and performance

Two things happen when you push the problem into the background and become engaged in some physical activity. You leave your state of frustration and enter into the state in which you enjoy doing this particular physical activity. That changes the thoughts available to you. At the same time, you allow more of your brain to be active, which creates the possibility of having new parts of your brain work on your problem.

As you engage in a physical activity you enjoy, your body takes on the physiology of someone who moves easily and effectively through the world. Your muscles warm up and loosen, your blood flows, and you take in a little more oxygen with each breath. You are moving freely and your body suggests to your mind that it can move freely too. Instead of being stuck mentally and free physically, your natural inclination is to be as free mentally as you are physically.

As your brain becomes active in many different centres (required to run your physical activity on both sides of your body), the neurological pattern for your activity becomes 'wired' into the problem solving that you left running in the background. The more of your brain is active, the more new connections are forming. You are almost literally putting a different part of your brain to work on your problem (that's not exactly how neurology works but it's a useful way of thinking about it). How effective this will be depends on how quickly you move from thinking about the problem to beginning the physical activity. It also depends on how deeply you have encoded the problem in your neurology (by going over it repeatedly or by experiencing strong emotion while thinking about it).

The next step is to test the results. You don't need to believe that physical activity will help you solve the problem. You just need to become active and then notice how your thinking about the problem changes. You might notice that you now have a potential solution. You might notice that you now enjoy working on the problem again. Or you might notice that the problem no longer feels like such a big deal. But you will only know what changes after you have taken the chance to do a dance, play a game or go for a walk.

A physical state solves the public speaking problem

One of the most famous techniques in NLP is the phobia cure. The founders of NLP made a name for themselves by claiming they could cure phobias in a matter of minutes. The fear of public speaking is certainly one of the world's most widespread phobias, and this could be a story about using the phobia cure to rid someone of that fear. But that would make it seem like the expert was the one who did battle with the fear.

I had a coaching client who we will call Ian. Ian was a professional engineer who was very good at his work and had founded a successful small business. Now he was reaching his limits as an entrepreneur, largely because he was afraid of public speaking. As he became more successful, the fear spread so that he was often intimidated by clients or colleagues in conversation. He called to ask me how long it would take to treat his problem. I asked how long he had been afraid of speaking. He said twenty years. I said it might take more than one session.

Ian met me with a mixture of hope and skepticism. During our opening conversation, I was looking for experiences that would help Ian to balance his habitual fear of speaking. I learned that he was a black belt in a martial art and that he had earned that black belt much more quickly than is usual by working one on one with a sensei. He had great muscle memory for exactly how he had to stand and balance to face an opponent and for how to pay attention so that he could anticipate his adversary's movements. We agreed that this was precisely the combination that would help him feel more at ease in speaking and he began to condition himself to use that muscle memory every time he was preparing to speak.

A month later, Ian returned to tell me that he had fine-tuned the state further so that he had exactly the combination of physiology and attention he required. While he had not yet done the public speaking for which he was preparing, he had already noticed that he was much more comfortable in conversations at work and also able to relax more effectively at home with his family. The change happened so fast because he already had a reliable, repeated experience of the state that would be most helpful to him. His expertise was what he needed to solve his problem and move past it. My role as practitioner was not to solve his problem, but to put two things together that he had thought were different. As often happens, when he used his control of his physical state to prime his attention, the problem simply disappeared.

Creating new choice through physical movement

The integration of mind and body means that every problem, no matter how intellectual or emotional that problem may seem, is also represented in our physical bodies. While we think of that problem, we take on postures, gestures and expressions that are part of how we represent the situation in our brains. When we make changes in our postures, gestures and attention, we open up new connections in our brains and we open up new paths to a solution.

Think of a problem that has been hard for you to solve. As you do, let the problem take up all your awareness so that it seems you are right in the middle of it. Notice what changes in your awareness. Are you more aware of pictures or sounds or feelings? As you work through your senses, are you aware of a still picture or a moving one? What are the qualities of the sounds you are hearing? Are they loud or soft, close or far, high-pitched or low, varied or monotone? And where are you aware of feelings in your body? You might notice tension or relaxation, coolness or warmth, tingling or twitching. Make a few notes of elements that seem important to you.

Now go sit in a different chair or stand in a different place. Look at your list and ask yourself, "when have I experienced something that is the exact opposite of this?" Whatever comes to mind, just let it be. Don't argue with yourself about whether or not it is the exact opposite. Trust yourself to have chosen something useful. Later you may understand why it is exactly right. For now, build up the experience in your mind as though it were happening now. Learn how it feels in your body and how it impacts your vision and hearing. Be so curious about every aspect that you would recognize this experience again just by the traces it leaves in your physiology.

Finally, put the two together. Go back to where you were sitting or standing at first and deliberately remember the second state. Use your notes if it helps you to shift your posture, gestures and attention so that you are in the second state while standing in the spot associated with the problem you have not yet solved. If a solution pops now, simply step away and put it to work. But if no solution pops, move back and forth between the two spots until you can stand or sit comfortably in the problem and maintain the physiology of the opposite state. At first you will notice that everything feels confused. That's because you have deliberately matched plaids and stripes. You have taken the physiology of one kind of experience and matched it with a completely different kind of experience. Your brain will notice the incongruence and begin to resolve it. After a few minutes, you will have found a way to comfortably combine the two very different experiences.

You will definitely notice you have a different sense of your own effectiveness and energy as you confront the problem. You might even notice that the problem is no longer that hard or no longer worth solving. If it is worth solving, you are likely to solve it almost without thinking about it.

Don't take my word for it. Test it out.

Three steps to problem solving with mind/body integration

1. Start from the assumption that your physiology and breathing are as much a part of your thinking as your logic or your gut reactions.

2. When you run into a problem you cannot solve, let go of logic and focus on what your body already knows. Find out how your body recognizes the problem.

3. Identify the physical cues associated with a more useful state. Practice until you can maintain that physical state while thinking of your problem. Within only a few moments, you might have the insight that will allow you to solve the problem with the greatest impact and the smallest expenditure of resources and energy.

Mind/body connections open up new possibilities

You already know something about how you connect with others in ways that are easy to do but hard to notice. This is what we mean by unconscious process. When you are paying attention to someone, you naturally fall into step with them as you walk; you naturally adjust your pace and posture to match them; you naturally change that pace when you want to make a point or change the direction of your conversation. It is obvious that we all make adjustments in response to other people and that we are only aware of making those adjustments some of the time. We think that the primary vehicle for shared meaning is our words. That's only partly true. You can remember a silence that marked a turning point in an interaction or a time when waiting was more useful than speaking.

You realize that other people are always influencing the way you move, breathe and speak and the qualities of your emotional state. Have you ever tried to stay relaxed while connecting with someone who is very tense? It should make sense to you that you are also having an influence on the people around you and that the most important part of that influence might come through your state and non-verbal communication. As you influence the way someone stands, moves, gestures or smiles, you also influence the way they will encounter you and the rest of the world for as long as your influence holds.

Tracking the real power in the circle

Many years ago, I was training a group of about eighteen people associated with a police service. All but one were police officers and fifteen of the eighteen were men (they included the head of the unit and the former head of the unit). The only civilian was a woman. While everyone else was in pants, she wore a skirt. She was bright, interested, and inconspicuous for most of the training. That changed when we did an exercise in non-verbal influence.

The assignment was that the entire group was to find and hold a posture that would be comfortable for everyone in the circle. No one was to speak until the exercise was complete. At first, various people tried exaggerated and somewhat aggressive postures. Some people would support them and some would move immediately into a counter posture. The woman in the skirt simply held her ground. She waited in a posture that would be comfortable for men in slacks and also comfortable and suitable for the skirt and shoes she was wearing. In the end, everyone matched her.

If you were in the room watching the power dynamics of the group as they unfolded over several days, you might have been confused by the authority of some participants and the agreement or disagreement evident in their words. You probably would have missed an important lesson in holding a congruent, non-threatening purpose in your body as clearly as you held it in your mind. I might have missed it too. But I would not miss it again.

Influence from the back of the room

Try this the next time you are in a room where someone else is the speaker. It might be a meeting, a class or a family gathering, as long as you choose a time when a vocal leader is present and everyone is gathered in one physical space. Now decide. Will you amplify the influence of someone else in the group or will you introduce a new element? Choose a state that you believe will lead to an optimal result for the gathering.

If you decide to amplify, simply match the posture, gestures and expressions of the person whose influence you are amplifying. If you decide to change the state or pace in the room, then begin by focusing on one other person to influence. Match that person only enough so that you feel like they are aware of your attention. Then move more solidly into the state you want to introduce.

Let your attention move to several other people in the room. Each time, allow yourself to non-verbally signal connection by matching elements of their non-verbal behaviour. Then move solidly into the state you want to spread throughout the room. From time to time, make a connection with the leader who is speaking. You will begin to notice that when you are attentive to the leader, the people with whom you have made a connection will also be attentive. Notice the other signs that people are accepting your non-verbal leadership and focusing on the way you are moving through the meeting.

Three steps to influence without saying a word

1. Influence begins with choosing the result you want. Know what state of mind and body you think will be useful and enter that state yourself.

2. Match the non-verbal behaviours of the person you want to influence just long enough to establish a connection.

3. Hold the state you decided would be useful and wait for the other person to join you there.

Setting goals through mind/body integration

There is an increasing body of research that says people are happier and more engaged when they have goals, and that goals are most achievable when they have been fully imagined using all the senses. In this case, NLP and the research are on the same page. Goals work best when they are positively framed, achievable, and fully imagined. And imagination is the part of our thinking that is tied most closely to our physical bodies. While "images" contain visual information, our imaginations work to create the semblance of reality by filling in an idea with information from all our senses. When we fully imagine a goal, we are more likely to create positive experiences by thinking about that goal, more likely to work towards the goal, and more likely to finally achieve it.

Mental rehearsal includes mind and body

As incredible as it still seems to many people, there is now evidence that thinking about our senses creates stimulation in the sensory centres in our brain and that vividly imagining something creates the same pattern of stimulation that would be created by actually experiencing the same thing (Doidge, 2007). Athletes and performers have often been taught to vividly imagine their performance as part of their preparation for important events. They know that mental rehearsal produces real results. Some studies show as much improvement in skills from mental rehearsal as can be achieved through actual physical practice. Neurologically, this has to do with the plasticity of the brain and the creation of neural patterns corresponding to the desired behaviours. On another level, mental rehearsal may be more easily understood as a joining of three critical forces: conscious intention, unconscious behaviours, and the functions of the body. Mental rehearsal requires all three parts of you. When your conscious mind, your unconscious processes and your body work together in pursuit of a goal, your best stuff is available for pursuing that goal.

Mental rehearsal means imagining you can see, hear, feel and move precisely the way you would during the performance of a particular skill or event. When you mentally rehearse achieving a goal, you prime your brain and your body to recognize and respond to the circumstances that will support that achievement. Goal setting with the mind and the body means that you don't just have the thought, "I would like this;" you actually rehearse the moment when you will have "this" and also any processes that you know will be necessary to get you to that moment.

Have you ever wanted a healthy snack but didn't get it because it seemed like too much work? Try this. Mentally rehearse everything you would have to do to put down this book and move to wherever you could purchase, pick up or make a healthy snack. Let your internal camera scan down to find you and watch you as you get up and move towards the location of the snack. Pan down to a different camera, this one in your own eyes, so that you see the room around you but only catch glimpses of your body. Begin to add in the sounds which are present in the environment and the sounds you make as you move. And then move your attention into your body and feel the muscles as they contract or lengthen, feel the stretch of your arms or the tightness as your legs change position. Move back out to the wide angle to watch yourself move again. Notice that you can only pay attention to one sense and one point of view at a time. You'll have to complete the circuit several times to capture all the information and a sense of how it all fits together as though you were actually moving now.

Now you can repeat that process to rehearse the moment when you realize you have achieved a goal you have been pursuing. Whatever your goal is, you want to be able to stabilize your representation of it so that you will recognize it when you achieve it. What will be true in your state, your behaviour and your environment at the moment when you realize you have achieved this thing you want? You'll get better responses to this question by watching it all unfold in your mind's eye than you would by filling out a long questionnaire. After all, each checkbox reminds you that you are working one piece at a time, but in life you experience all five senses, your physical feelings and your thoughts at precisely the same time.

You are the director of your life story

I have a friend who is a theatre director. He directs about one play each year, and it takes him almost the whole of the year to prepare for that one play's run. What does he do before rehearsals start? He mentally rehearses his goal for that play. He uses various techniques to imaginatively live in the world of the play and then to move with the actors on stage during a performance and then to sit in the audience and watch the whole of the play unfold before him. His goal for the performances does not fit conveniently into a phrase or a sentence. It's not even easy to contain in a full proposal. The real goal is expressed fully only in his imagination as he watches and tweaks and watches again. He begins even before he knows what the stage or the actors will look like and he continues even as a performance begins. By then he cannot help it. His imagining of the experience of the goal has been conditioned so that it starts to run whenever he thinks about the play.

Your life goals are worth the same attention my director friend gives to his play. It is worth imagining what you want from different perspectives using different strengths and techniques. Along the way, you will condition yourself so that any external experience related to your goal automatically leads to you adding new information to the way you imagine achieving the goal. Making the goal real begins to feel inevitable as you notice opportunities and weave them into a fully imagined experience of your goal.

Develop a fully-imagined goal

Creating fully imagined goals is a skill to be practiced. Begin with something with well-defined limits. Think, perhaps, of a meal you would like to prepare, a special evening you would like to experience, or a room you would like to redecorate. If all of these still seem overwhelming, imagine picking just one piece of furniture to add to your home or just one routine project to complete at work. Whatever you pick, it needs to already exist in your memory in some form. It's easiest to start with a dish you have already made or a task you have already done.

Once you have decided on a goal, practice making it vivid in your imagination. First make a picture with you at the centre at the moment you achieve your goal. Look around and see where you are and when you are and how you are related to the people or things around you. Switch to a second camera so that now you are looking out through your own eyes. Notice what looks different from this viewpoint. Then become aware of sounds: the ones around you and the voice in your head at the moment when you succeed at your goal. Finally let your attention drop into your body and notice as much as you can about your physiology at this moment. Think about what you notice on or through your skin, your muscles, your breathing, your heartbeat and balance, the small muscles on your face.

Now go back in time and starting from where you are right now, make a movie of how you decided to set this goal and all the things you did to make it happen. The movie ends back at that scene you have just mentally rehearsed, the moment of achievement. There may be gaps in the narrative where the screen goes dark and then opens onto a different time or place. That's okay. It's your movie. The key is to get a big picture view of what you will have to do and what others will have to do if you are to achieve what you want to achieve. Just watch the movie with lots of curiosity, adding sound and physical sensation whenever that seems helpful.

Finally, plan for the next time you will sit down and mentally rehearse for this goal. If it's going to take more than a few days to achieve, you will want to rehearse every day or two. Watching yourself rehearse in the future is a great way to make it likely that you will remember to keep practicing.

Three steps for using mind/body integration to set goals

1. When you find yourself saying or deciding that you want something, do a quick scan of your body, your expressions and your behaviour. You'll know if they are all in agreement. If they are, you're ready to make this goal more compelling.

2. When you want something congruently, the full range of your perceptions, memories, abilities and strengths are available to help you achieve it. Take time to mentally rehearse for the result you want.

3. Do you want to be exhausted, elated or matter-of-fact when you achieve this goal? Build the state you want into your imagining of the goal so that you will not just get what you want, you'll also like the way you feel when you get it.

People Have What They Need

It's easy to be overwhelmed by all the things that can go wrong and all the very good reasons to believe that people are stuck, that situations are hopeless, that there are not enough resources for people to be well and fulfilled and happy. In some cases, it may be true. The deck may be stacked against you or against someone you would like to help. The odds are not always in our favour.

The truth is that realistic appraisals have their place, but they are ultimately less useful than optimism. For reasons that are not entirely clear, when people believe good things are possible, they often make good things happen. Sometimes they change the situation and sometimes they change their perceptions, but they become more satisfied. In NLP, this idea goes back to the work of Milton Erickson and is a foundation of NLP techniques. In order to use the techniques effectively, you have to act as though you believe that everyone has within them the perceptions and abilities necessary to live a more satisfying life.

This means that in applying NLP to your own life you simply assume that you have what you need and just need to find it. Whatever your problem, whether you are in pain, confused, stuck or in pursuit of a goal that seems impossible, the only problem from an NLP point of view is that you have not yet made a connection between that situation and the appropriate resources. Making new connections opens up new possibilities in the relationship between you and this problem or goal. Sometimes you will change and sometimes your goal will change so that the new relationship is more satisfying to you.

Getting to the resources beyond the pain

Whether your pain is physical or emotional, it is manipulative. It can occupy so much of your conscious attention that it feels as though pain is the whole of your world. This is as true in cases of depression as it is of migraine headaches or businesses on the verge of bankruptcy. It's as though pain takes control of our perceptual processes so that it can monopolize our conscious awareness. This is one of the reasons we so often turn to other people for help with our pain. Their attention moves through a wider frame and they can see around and over and past our pain in a way that we cannot. Dealing with pain begins with knowing that there is more to our experience than the pain that is preoccupying us at the moment. Managing pain depends on accessing the resources in all of the experience that is shut out of consciousness while we pay attention to pain.

NLP distracts the attention from the pain and then explores strengths, experiences and beliefs that can come to mind once the pain no longer controls all of the perceptual field. In the relative freedom provided by distraction, people make connections to the parts of themselves (or their businesses) that the pain made invisible. This may do two things. Sometimes the new connections are strong enough to change the experience of pain. Sometimes the new connections prime unconscious processes to develop a way to work around the pain. All pain cannot be eliminated, but all people can know themselves as separate from their pain and see the whole of their experience in a frame that includes pain without being defined by it.

Could you play with your pain?

Oddly, when we think of something as being 'a pain' we do not mean that it is painful, so much as that it is an irritation. Irritation, like pain, tends to overwhelm conscious attention so that it does not have sufficient resources to simultaneously think about other things and respond to the irritation. For many people, seasonal allergies are not painful, but they are 'a pain' and they work the same way that pain does to overwhelm and block out better possibilities.

I have had seasonal allergies for most of my life. When I was only seven, I was visiting family friends and spent a miserable weekend fending off headaches and congestion and sneezes. When I was a graduate student, I took old-fashioned antihistamines that made me so drowsy that finishing my thesis took place in a kind of haze. At no time was I overwhelmed by pain because of allergies, but I was often uncomfortable and distracted. It became a dangerous problem in the summers just before I started NLP, when my eyes would become itchy and inflamed and then water copiously. It made it difficult to drive comfortably and safely.

When I took my NLP Practitioner training, we came to an exercise the trainer promised would make it impossible to enter a state ever again. This exercise was so powerful that when you completed it, that particular pain would be gone forever. "Right," I thought. "I will play along." I could think of no good reason for my eyes to sting and water uncontrollably, and I decided to take that as the state to eliminate through this exercise. At no point did I believe that playing a silly game could possibly change a biochemical condition that had been plaguing me for years. But I played the game.

The game itself was designed to allow participants to personify the problem or pain as a creature that snuck up on them, the kind of monster that jumps out from the shadows or appears behind your back. I was unimpressed, but I dutifully began by imagining that my eyes were watering (they weren't), stepped away and played the game. I am not particularly good at improv games, but when I agree to do something visibly foolish in a public park, I generally decide to ham it up a little. Why go 70% of the way when you could go all in? So I did. I played the game, and at the end, I jumped into the space where I had left the problem. And my eyes did not water. Of course, they hadn't been watering at the beginning either. As quickly as possible, I put the whole thing out of my mind.

Within a relatively short time, I began to co-train NLP programs, and not long after that, to train on my own. When I came to this part of the course, I was quite anxious about how I would pull it off. After all, I didn't believe it would work; it made me feel ridiculous; and I expected lots of resistance from my students. That was the first time I checked in with myself and realized, two years later, that my eyes had stopped watering uncontrollably during allergy season.

It is harder than you might think to notice when a problem disappears. When it's gone, your field of perception fills up with other information and you begin to explore new territory. There's not much attention left to cycle back and ask, "wasn't there something else here?" At first, I would have thought there was a change in the weather, my mind, my driving pattern. Perhaps there was. I only know that I had a problem, I played a game, and the problem stopped.

Since my realization, this has become an exercise that long-time clients request, a game clients become intensely engaged with playing.

Somewhere in the pattern is something primal: a recognition that if you could only step away from pain and creep up on it, explore it safely from new angles and positions, and be brave and focused in its face, then perhaps you could also make it disappear from your awareness.

How to tame a pain

If you are in a lot of pain, physical or emotional, then you will probably find it takes much training, willpower and discipline to manage it yourself. It's not impossible, but it is not a task for beginners. You can discover what is possible by beginning with an irritation, a pain that distracts you from other things but is not intolerable.

If the pain is physical, work on it using imagination. If it is emotional, work on it using physical movement. Your first goal is to discover that you can be distracted from the pain. For physical pain, try movies, music or meditation. For emotional pain try a workout, a walk or housework. When you become aware of the pain, simply notice that you must have been distracted from it (otherwise it would not have popped back into your awareness) and be curious about what must be true in yourself, your behaviour and your environment for you to be distracted from pain.

The next step is to begin to 'call your shots.' In this instance, it means actually stating your intention whether you are engaging with your pain, stepping away from it, or doing something else. For instance, a typical monologue might be, "My head hurts behind my right eye. I am going to separate myself from the pain in my head. Now I am walking and I am noticing the fresh air, the sunshine, the sidewalk under my shoes, the children playing in that driveway. For a moment I noticed my headache, and then I decided to breathe with my walking, four steps in, four steps out." Begin to notice that the 'you' who is calling the shots is not the same 'you' as the head that hurts.

This widens the frame so that you can perceive your headache, the whole of you, and the space around you. Now begin to remember yourself in times and places where there was no headache. Pick one that you particularly enjoy and go there in your imagination. If you are working with an emotional pain, pick a favourite place and physically go there. Move around this place (whether imagined or physically present) and tell yourself what you love about it. If you find you completely lose track of the pain and get caught up in doing something you enjoy, that's great. If not, tell yourself that you will sneak up on this pain so that it cannot sneak up on you again.

Begin to test your ability to occupy the same space as the pain without feeling the pain. As soon as you notice even a twinge, move back into an awareness of good things around you or places of comfort within you. Let your resourcefulness build up, and then slide back into the space of the pain for just a fraction of a second. Test your ability to remain comfortable until you don't need to test it anymore. You are just comfortable.

The key to this is to invest as little attention as possible in the thing that causes you pain. Notice the pain just enough so that you can notice when it is gone.

Three steps to resourcefulness for people in pain

1. It's hard to be at your best when you are in pain. Whenever possible, say yes to help. Some help will come from your knowledge of what has given you comfort before, whether it means tea and toast in bed, a mindless movie, or a special treat for dessert.

2. Some help will come from professionals; it's good to talk to your doctor, coach, therapist or another support person.

3. Other help will come from people who love you. Let someone else look after you or look after some of your chores. You will find that it is helpful to counter the voice in your head that says you deserve to be in pain with the voice of someone you respect who does not believe you deserve to be in pain and does not believe you will stay there for long.

Knowing You Have the Next Piece of the Puzzle

Have you ever wondered how people keep themselves motivated to work on problems they may never solve? It's an interesting question for people who study motivation. What keeps scientists working to discover a new drug when most of them will never bring a product to market? We could ask the same thing about activists fighting poverty or disease. What keeps them going when they'll never find 'the answer?'

The trick in solving big problems seems to be the same trick that allows people to solve more limited puzzles. You need to believe that you have something that will allow you to find or contribute to the next step. Whether the next step is a tiny increment of the progress you need or the big leap that solves the problem, you start in the same place. You start with the belief that it's worth looking in your thoughts and experiences for a resource that will lead to a solution. You cannot know you can solve the problem but the only way to solve it is to pretend there is an answer within reach and look for it in the only places you can access: your own experience and knowledge.

Human neurology works by making connections between a new stimulus and the experiences stored in memory. The brain connects the new to the old and either extends or modifies what it knows. If there is not enough connection, the new stimulus cannot be interpreted or remembered. If you are paying attention to a problem, you have already decided that there is some connection between that problem and your knowledge and experience. Either the connection you have made will offer a perspective or information that solves the problem or you will need to try a different connection, to make a different analogy or to work on the problem from a new perspective. If you hit on the best connection quickly, you may leap to a solution. If your first connections do not work, then you can systematically work through other connections to make progress towards a solution. Once you really believe that there is a connection between your knowledge and ability and the problem you wish to solve, you will be motivated to continue to try new connections until you are satisfied by your progress.

Believe you have the answers when you write the test

There are many people who will tell you that hypnosis or NLP can be used to improve your memory as you study. Like many claims that there is a short route to success, that one is partly true. What's reliably true is that you are more likely to be able to access what you know when you write a test if you have a) done the work to learn the material and b) believe that you will be able to access your knowledge at the appropriate time and place. This belief not only works during the examination, it also motivates you to pay attention more effectively while you study.

When my son was preparing for the LSAT (the Law School Admissions Test), he asked me to do a coaching session with him and a study partner. My approach to helping involved two steps: 1) to work with techniques that serve as mental rehearsal so that clients enter their strongest state as they enter the exam room and 2) to allow them to connect with their own best appraisal of what they knew and what they still needed to prepare so that they would be successful while writing the examination. The essence of the approach is that the role of the coach is to ensure that clients have the motivation to do appropriate preparation and then are able to walk into a test congruently knowing that they have what they need to succeed.

The key to this was establishing a relaxed, open focus to access an unconscious evaluation of what was necessary to complete preparations. It's not that the unconscious is a wise alter-ego who can be mysteriously summoned to prophesy. The unconscious simply assembles, relates, and makes meaning from more information than can be handled in conscious awareness. I asked my son if he knew what he needed to do so that he could be fully prepared. The response he gave through unconscious signals was that he was not yet ready but he did know what else he needed to do.

Later that week, my son emailed to say that he was not sure the coaching session had helped because he was getting lower scores on practice tests. I stuck to my belief that clients have the resources they need and told him that was his way of focusing his efforts on the material he needed to know better before he wrote the exam. Was it true? There is no way of knowing, but he did very well on the test. He got the result he wanted, so we do know that he was able to do the work he needed to do and that he was able to access the results of that work under pressure.

Identify new resources to apply to your problem

You might think metaphor is something you left behind in school, a vaguely-remembered literary technique that had something to do with courage being like a lion or love being like a rose. Metaphor is a literary technique but it is also a way of thinking that is so natural it seems to be hard-wired into our brains. When we talk about feeling down or up, when we talk about problems being hard, and when we talk about making mountains out of molehills, we are using metaphor to explore or define the relationship between something real and something abstract. It gives us an intuitive way to take abstract problems and work on them using information that is satisfyingly concrete. The key to metaphor is to stay with it until it points you to the resources you already have that will allow you to solve the problem.

Begin by thinking of a problem you are currently working to solve. Ask yourself, does this remind me of a vehicle, an animal, or a place in my neighborhood? Don't ask yourself why it reminds you of this, but do notice that the only way to generate an answer is to access some of the perceptions you have about the problem that were probably outside your awareness until you asked yourself the question.

Now forget about the problem and explore the metaphor. For instance, you might be working on a really tough situation in which you find little hope. Your metaphor would reflect this. Maybe what comes to mind is a documentary you watched about elephants walking hundreds of miles across desolate plains to get to water. That's a great start. Now let's explore it.

Who are you in your metaphor? In the elephant example, are you one of the elephants, a bird flying overhead, or one of the small animals displaced as the herd thunders by? If you picked a vehicle, are you the vehicle, the driver, a passenger or someone watching? Notice how quickly you are sketching in characteristics and relationships as you make these choices. You should continue to develop the metaphor until you know how the different players in the problem fit into the metaphor, how energy and support work within metaphor (what do elephants eat?), and how the environment both supports and hurts the vehicles, animals or inhabitants.

The metaphor will give you new perspectives on your problem to the extent that you are willing to explore the metaphor as real and not abstract. For instance, you may think that seeing yourself as a lion means you are a noble leader. That's not thinking in metaphor. Thinking in metaphor tells you that a lion sleeps most of the day, surrounds himself with strong females and sees other males as adversaries to be fought or controlled. Your metaphors will not always communicate ideas you like. You are exploring them to think about a situation you do not like and resources you have not yet noticed you have. The information you need to unlock new perspectives and resources will sometimes trigger your resistance. That's okay. In fighting with your own metaphor, you will also discover new information.

The key to a useful metaphor is that it feels both familiar and surprising. You may feel uncomfortable at first, as though analysis were the only legitimate way of approaching a difficult problem. When you work through that, you will find what many of the world's most inventive scientists have found. Exploring the metaphor with an open mind will lead to surprisingly useful results.

Three steps to knowing you have what you need to solve the problem

1. Do the work required. You have to study for the exam. You have to prepare the analysis for the report. You have to practice for the performance. The belief that you are resourceful is meant to support you in preparation, not to replace it.

2. Connect with someone who holds strongly to the belief that you will find what you need to solve your problem. Knowing that someone we respect believes we have done the work well enough to succeed can make it easier to hold onto that belief ourselves.

3. Think metaphorically. The more sensory information you can add to a problem, the more likely you are to find new perspectives and strengths.

Win by bringing out the best in other people

There are at least two ways to think about influence. The first is to see it as a zero-sum game where your win is someone else's loss. This model is the old-fashioned con game where one person (smart) targets another (gullible) and takes something. The other way to think about influence is quite different. It's a model that says our ability to influence one another is so innate that it must have evolutionary advantage. In this model, influence is the way we bring out the best in each other to create more value together than we would have individually. Whether the influence is framed as teaching, managing, or sales, the aim is to create value so that everyone wins.

If you would like to win and create value for the people you influence, then one part of your method must be to elicit resourcefulness in those people. When you show people they really are stronger than they think, you demonstrate why two heads are better than one and influence can actually create value. Whether your role is explicitly one-way influence (teaching, sales, managing, etc.) or collaborative, it's useful to approach people in a way that allows them to discover new resources in themselves or their position.

At the heart of this is the ability to notice when you are congruent about your approach and when others are congruent in receiving your influence. When you are congruent, your ability to calibrate is at its peak. This means you are able to accurately identify the meaning of changes you notice in the people you influence. When they are congruent, they are engaged consciously and unconsciously by your lead and are most likely to discover new resources in themselves or in your shared situation.

Discover resources in difficult groups to lead

Do you know the expression 'herding cats?' Even if you don't, you probably have an instant visual of what that would be like and so you know what it means. Many leadership challenges feel like herding cats, as if you were working against nature to create order and flow in creatures that are naturally difficult, independent and curious.

Look what happened in that final statement and you'll have a clue to discovering resources in the people you are leading or influencing. It begins by describing cats as "difficult" and moves to "independent" and "curious." The final two are qualities that are useful in many contexts. Within a few words, we have reframed our vision of cats from negative (they make our task difficult) to positive (they are engaged in their own stuff and curious about ours).

Engaging college students can be like herding cats

This is the reframe I do each time I step into a classroom of college students. In the college where I teach, students are required to bring laptops to class and they sit in pods of four, facing each other and within sight of multiple screens. Most of them have smart phones on the desk next to their computers and many of them are wearing headsets. Floor to ceiling windows invite them to look outside the room. It is hard to imagine that the whole class could ever pay attention to just one thing, much less that the one thing could be the teacher's message.

My students need to be able to filter the overflow of information to identify where they want to pay attention. This will be a core skill for getting things done in this class, in other classes, and in their careers. The price of admission for me as a teacher is to believe that they are capable of offering me enough of their attention for learning to happen.

The most important distraction in the room is never technological and is usually not apparent at first glance. Students often do not know that they are capable of shutting down the noise and paying attention. When they begin to filter out the phones and music and instant messaging, they confront their fear that they will not be good at what I will ask them to do. I engage them because I imagine two things that are hard for them to believe themselves: that they are capable of paying attention as a group and that they will be capable of doing the work. This takes imagining. Neither thing is necessarily true. It also takes a strong sense of purpose. Because I am there to teach, I believe they are there to learn and I act as if that were true.

Remarkably, it is often true. As long as I hold the belief that my students are more capable than they appear, they are often able to surprise themselves with their ability to interact and communicate effectively. One day, I noticed a young woman with her head on her desk and her eyes closed. Instead of reprimanding her, I said, "You look really tired. It must have been hard to get yourself to class today." She arrived early (wide awake) the next week and participated more actively than ever before. This was not a major turning point, but it is one example of how acting as if people have resources often allows them to act as if they had those resources. The bonus is that they are also likely to associate you with the resourcefulness you help them uncover in themselves.

Influence from the inside out

You can discover the subtlety with which people can be influenced if you pick someone to be a model and allow that person to influence you. This gives you new information about what others will experience as you influence them. Look around and choose someone you believe has a strength, skill or characteristic that would be useful to you. Pretend that you are an actor who will play this person in a movie or television show. To prepare for the role, you must be able to replicate both their obvious behaviours and the thoughts, beliefs and emotions that are characteristic of them.

To do this, you will retrieve one of your earliest learning behaviours. Small children practice by pretending to be someone who has the ability they want. They might choose a superhero, a performer, or an athlete as their model. They imagine that they can dress as their model dresses, move as their model moves, speak as their model speaks, and often, lead as their model leads. You will probably not want to turn a tea towel into a superhero cape, but you do want to enter into imagining your model with all the playfulness of a child.

Begin by noticing obvious behaviours: walk, talk, habits. You can mentally rehearse how it would feel to enter a room as your model does, to lead a meeting as your model does, to encounter other people with the same expressions and attitudes as your model does. You might even find that you are unconsciously adopting some of these behaviours in a way that feels appropriate to you.

Now move to the reason you chose this model, the skill or characteristic that the model has that you wish you had. Whether it's a way of analyzing a business opportunity or of swinging a golf club, take every opportunity to watch your model do this thing in the same way that a professional athlete might analyze video of a particular performance. Be curious about everything. You want to play this person accurately right down to the last detail. Later you can decide which choices, attitudes or steps are essential to getting the result you want. First, sit somewhere quiet and run the video in your mind as though you were seeing through your model's eyes; speaking with your model's voice, and noticing what your model notices.

At some point, you will want to do that thing that your model does so well. You will have a chance to notice what has changed in the way you approach and perform this particular skill or how well you are able to create and maintain this particular characteristic. Other people may notice and comment on changes in your approach or ability, or perhaps you will notice that you are getting a result more easily or more effectively.

Three steps to uncover resourcefulness in others

1. Paying attention to someone's strength allows us to see them at their best. When we do, they become more aware of the best in themselves.

2. Push aside doubts and difficulties and simply pretend that you can be like someone you admire in some respect.

3. Pretend that anyone you want to influence might also have something to share with you, a gift or strength that you will notice because of the attention you pay while you are exploring the best way to connect and move together.

KNOW WHAT YOU REALLY WANT

In his 2009 exhibition, *Massive Change*, Bruce Mau asked the question, "Now that we can do anything, what do we want to do?" This is a version of the question that we face when we accept that we have what we need to be more satisfied with our lives. "Now that I can have what I really want, what do I want?" It's a big question that suggests that if we are not satisfied it is because we have not chosen our goals wisely.

At the heart of NLP is a belief that we can always want something that will make our experience better. We are never without choices, so what we choose matters. We must nurture our own resourcefulness and weave it into the goals we set so that we create the best possible outcomes, over and over again. Instead of investing in wishes that will never come true, we have both the opportunity and the responsibility to frame goals that will lead to a life well-lived.

Want is a word with two meanings. On the one hand, to want something means to desire it. On the other hand, wanting can also mean missing something necessary. We carry both meanings into the goals we set. Something we want is something we desire and yet when we agree to desire it, we acknowledge our life is currently missing something. If we want impossible things, then we doom ourselves to lives of wanting (missing a necessary ingredient). If we don't want anything, then we stop growing. It is reassuring to begin from a presupposition that we can find what is missing and that even if we do not find it, wanting it can lead to a more satisfying life.

If we have within us what we need to lead satisfying lives, it must follow that we have within us what we need to form the kind of goals that enrich our lives, both while we pursue them and when we achieve them.

Set goals that are just beyond your limits

Research on goals suggest that the best policy is to set a goal that is just beyond your limits, something that you are not sure to achieve but are likely to achieve (Bannink, p.86). This would be easy if goals came with sticker prices, but they do not. We are not always sure what our limits are and we cannot control the changes in the environment that will influence our achievements.

The answer in NLP and other solution-focused techniques is to imagine a desired future with such detail that it begins to feel less like a fantasy and more like a memory. If a goal is easily achieved, we are unlikely to imagine it this way. It will be less trouble just to go out and make it real. If a goal is too difficult, we are likely to find big holes in our imagining. So a goal that we can imagine fully is likely to be a goal that is just right.

What we are doing when we mentally rehearse an achievement is a kind of practice. There is now abundant evidence that mental rehearsal affects the way the brain handles the thing we are rehearsing. It dedicates more neurons to the processes necessary to do this thing and it creates pathways that are more resilient in its representation of the achievement. The result of mental rehearsal is that we know what we want and what we need to do to make it happen; we recognize opportunities in the environment more often; and we are able to take reliable action more quickly in response to those opportunities.

In effect, when we mentally rehearse we are creating a memory of something that has not yet happened. A memory is a stored pattern that represents the whole of a situation as it will be lived in our thoughts, our senses and our bodies. The brain can compare this pattern to sensory information and prompt appropriate action when opportunities appear. Often this action happens 'without thinking.' We automatically notice what we need to notice and do what we need to do to apply the pattern to our experience. Like other memories, our goals are encoded more strongly when we repeat our mental rehearsal and when we rehearse with more emotional intensity.

Some of the things we want are relatively new arrivals in our neurology. We are aware of the pattern we are setting; we rehearse it with intensity and we consciously benchmark and monitor our progress towards these goals. We know what we want and we have some idea how our perceptions and behaviours contribute to achieving what we want.

There are other patterns stored in our neurology, often patterns that have been there for some time. They are goals that got put on the back burner, so to speak. Many of them involve personal relationships (with partners, children, friends or parents) or identity (this is the kind of person I choose to be). At some point after we formed these goals, they seemed impossible. They may have been interrupted by trauma or been contradicted by a stronger goal. Over months or years, these memories get pushed aside so that we no longer think of them consciously. If, however, changes in our experience or environment begin to reactivate these patterns, we may end up pursuing goals we think we have outgrown or given up.

The path to your goals is not a straight line

What my clients want often surprises me. Several years ago, I trained Brian. Brian was a high-performer who had managed top grades and extra-curricular excellence throughout high school and university. He was now several years out of school and pursuing a career and family with the same passion for achievement. What surprised me was that his current goal was home ownership and yet he had invested in expensive training with dollars that could have gone towards a down payment. I was not surprised that four weeks later, after applying every aspect of the training to this one goal, Brian was negotiating the purchase of his first house.

The path that led him to that purchase was not a straight line. After he invested in training while saving for a down payment, he found the house he wanted through a network of friends. Someone was leaving a house in an area he liked, and he was able to negotiate a private purchase that brought the price within his range. It seemed that as his focus on the goal became clearer, the world arranged itself to meet him halfway. That's often the way it seems when we heighten our determination and the clarity of our vision. We notice opportunities that we assume were never available before (but maybe they were and we just didn't notice).

Leila, on the other hand, came to training with a stated desire for a new career. We talked before she registered about the transition she wanted to make and she explained why she wanted to make the change and how our training would move her forward. She didn't have a clear vision of where she would end up and she showed a preference for going into situations blind and exploring rather than planning. Not surprisingly, she enjoyed the training very much and made some changes, but they did not lead her into the career transition she had discussed. Instead, she made other moves and eventually I learned she had made peace with a sister from whom she had been estranged for many years. The 'want' that she filled was an old one, much better established than the one she was able to articulate before taking the training.

Both clients got something they wanted. Both took the training primarily for work reasons and yet, when invited to choose goals to work on, they chose to work mostly with changes to their personal lives. And both found that by working on the goals that came to mind they were able to discover that they did have all the resources they needed to do something that seemed beyond reach.

Nurture your own goals

When you are working with other people, it is relatively easy to uncover their hidden strengths. By holding the belief that the necessary resources will come to the surface, you assume that each person is already more than you know. Combining curiosity about what resources will be uncovered with a presupposition that new resources will appear makes it inevitable that in some way you will learn something that will serve the person whom you are observing.

The trick to doing this for yourself is to move into that watchful self that is separate from what W. B. Yeats once called the "bundle of accident and incoherence that sits down to breakfast" (*A General Introduction for My Work*, 1937). It's true that it can take years of meditation practice to get good at splitting your attention this way. It's also true that moving back and forth through a trusted, stabilized process allows you to capture more than you expect. For most people, this will involve writing, although audio or video recordings or images may also be used to take you simultaneously outside yourself (as writing or other productions are outside you) and inside yourself.

The trick to writing your goal is to write about it until you say something that surprises you and that feels absolutely true and right. Some people do this by adding layers of sensory data to the goal (describe what you will see, hear and feel when you achieve this thing you want). Some people do it by telling a story of how the goal was achieved (jump forward in time to the day after you achieve the goal and write the story of how you got to that day). Others do it by tracing the relationship of one goal to more abstract aspirations or beliefs (this goal is necessary to satisfy my knowledge of who I really am). If you are not good with writing, you may prefer to capture this kind of thinking in a recording, map, picture or collage. The key is to produce a level of detailed imagining that allows you to see something that you didn't consciously know you knew about yourself or your path.

As you shape a goal, you may want to consider how it is related to those things that all people need and want. Consider this: all human beings must satisfy both mind and body. Damaging one to serve the other is never sustainable for very long. The one that is being sacrificed will pull attention away from the one that is being served. Similarly, all human beings want to shape their own lives (autonomy) and yet also to connect with others (relationship). Take a blank piece of paper and draw a line down the middle of the page from top to bottom. Label the top 'Mind' and the bottom 'Body.' Draw a line across the middle of the page from the left to the right. Label the left 'Independence' and the right 'Relationships.' Ask yourself, "which of these quadrants is most full as I look at my life now?" Then ask, "which of these quadrants requires my attention for the whole of my life to be satisfying?"

The quadrant model is useful because it reminds us that no one goal will ever satisfy all parts of us, and those parts of us that we are not giving attention probably hold resources that we do not know and cannot use until we focus our attention in the service of a new goal. Make a list of ten or twelve goals that you are currently pursuing or want to pursue. Place each of them in one or more quadrants on the chart. What new information do you uncover about how your life is balanced in the productive tension between these drives?

Three steps to discover your hidden resources

1. As you hold one of your goals in your mind, you will find that you already have a good idea whether or not you are committed to achieving that goal. It is more likely that you will achieve the goals that feel congruent.

2. The resources we need to lead more satisfying lives are always available when we are willing to listen to the conversation between our minds, our hearts and our bodies. Congruence is the clue that shows us where we are hiding the best of ourselves.

3. It is not possible to be congruent at all times. Many tasks require that our attention move between different places or track different things. When you are not getting results you like, it is time to shut down the multiple streams, get congruent, and get in touch with new resources.

Moving on Common Ground

People are uniquely well-equipped to pay attention to other people. Whether by design or by evolution, our neurology is exquisitely developed for observing other human beings and predicting their behaviours. This makes sense because human beings are born into a world where they will need other people for several years before they become at all independent. This also makes sense because most human beings will step into a world where other human beings pose the greatest threat to their well-being. We are born to observe and predict the behaviours of the people around us.

This is one of the two most important truths about our neurological function. The other truth is that we can only learn by building on what we already know. Everything that is to be permanently stored in our memories must attach itself to a pattern that already exists there. We can't create a fresh start. We can only add to what we remember. Long-term access to what we add to memory is facilitated either by repetition or by emotional impact, but strong emotions attach themselves to pre-existing patterns. We learn by adding to what we already know.

When we put these two truths together, we realize at once that our ability to make positive, intentional change depends on our ability to find and navigate common ground with our past selves (who made the memories on which we build) and common ground with people around us (who provide the most direct route to new patterns of information or behaviour). Our emotions seem to have evolved to support the drive to move on common ground. When we connect well with others it supports the state of energized, relaxed focus associated with optimal learning and peak performance. When we do not connect well with others, distrust or incongruence blocks our ability to add their patterns to our own. Even when we are not consciously aware of whether or not we are moving on common ground, our intuitions and emotions are sending signals because parts of our neurology are tracking how we are similar to or different from the people with whom we are interacting.

It is always tempting to believe that we only have one path to follow at a time and we are able to forge that path through virgin territory. This is not likely to be true geographically and it is even less likely to be true intellectually. It's better to imagine that any new path we take is continually joining and leaving the paths followed by others. We choose a path that begins where we are and moves in the direction we want to go, at least for a while. The steps we take on a shared path are more certain, take less effort and lead to more predictable places.

In this chapter, we'll explore two kinds of common ground: the kind that exists in your brain between the experience you are having now and the patterns that you have stored in memory and the kind that exists between you and the people around you. You will find that both kinds of common ground are necessary to your ability to formulate outcomes and take reliable action whether your goal is to heal, to solve a problem, to connect with others or to set a new direction. Far from being a boring imitator of other people's leadership, the person who can navigate on common ground becomes the explorer with the best map and the leader with the best team.

Is a chronic illness a frenemy?

Have you heard the word 'frenemy?' It describes both friends that hurt us and enemies that help us. Think about this in terms of an illness that causes you ongoing stress and pain. It's obvious that the illness will become your adversary, but it may be necessary for it also to become a kind of friend. Frenemy might be the best description of your ideal relationship.

Could you fight a chronic illness? Probably not. That's why it's chronic. Could you ignore it? Again, probably not. If you could ignore it, you would already be ignoring it. Could you resent it? Of course you will resent it, but then you have also sometimes resented family or friends. It's only natural to resist the limitations that you feel when you are given no choice but to move on common ground with a chronic illness. The part of you that hosts the illness and the parts of you that are ambitious for change share the same body. They have to move together if they are to move at all. It's as awkward to move forward resenting that as it would be for your left and right legs to move in different directions.

What would it mean to make friends with a condition that is actively hurting you? The common ground should never be based on the hurt. But every illness moves your attention in ways that might be useful if they didn't hurt and every illness can prompt coping strategies that become common ground for other kinds of healing or problem-solving. This is the truth behind the media reports where someone says that getting cancer was the best thing that ever happened to them. The pain and the destruction you experience through the illness are different than the whole of you that experiences more than the illness. You will find common ground when you are able to accept that interacting with the illness has changed you in useful ways.

This is also true of whatever you want to heal now. As much as you want to give up what is hurting you, you want to begin by gently uncovering where you have room to move. Healing is more than the absence of pain: it's the ability to grow again. That means you need to do more than cut yourself off from the source of pain. You also have to preserve the part of you that has coped with the pain (possibly for many years) and the strengths you have developed as a result of that coping. You might feel consciously as though you would gladly trade those in for relief, but that is not how the equipment works. There is no fresh start and no pretending that you were never hurt in the first place. Instead, you have to connect what comes next to what needs to heal. And you do that best when you identify the strongest place to make the connection.

Choose to respect the self that failed you

Personal edits are techniques to transform a situation in which no choice seems possible, an experience of being stuck or cornered or inadequate in some way. The techniques are so appealing because they all use some combination of imagination and movement to allow a client to dissociate from the experience of being stuck. With the help of the trainer or coach and the process, clients get to simply walk away from the self that couldn't find a satisfactory choice.

The point of the dissociation is to allow a recognition of the many strengths, resources and capabilities that the individual can access when the pressure is off. The client may get pumped full of excitement and daring and creativity and the power of playing with scary stuff. This process can be tricky (if the dissociation is not complete) but it is essentially very nurturing. Some of the techniques might feel ridiculous (like an improv workshop) but they also feel good (like an improv workshop). And as they proceed, the client begins to feel more powerful and more clever and more whole than the self that was stuck.

The key to real change comes at the moment when the client confronts the old self, the stuck self, the self that let them down. Every exercise culminates in the instruction to move back into that self and integrate the resourcefulness into the situation which is still being played out internally, the situation where the choices available are not good enough. In theory, it's an easy step. In practice, many people cheat, at least a little. Freed from the self they didn't like very much in the first place, they choose to walk away without reintegrating. They keep the good stuff, and they lose the history.

As we have seen, you cannot really lose the history. It's real and it's persistent and it cannot be changed and it cannot be lost. My favourite moment in each training is the moment I watch as someone decides to own their past. That's the moment when a client is brave enough and resourceful enough to integrate the version of themselves that let them down. Some people call it identity, the recognition that we needed every bit of our history, good and bad, to get to the current moment. Some people call it forgiveness when they are able to embrace a part of themselves that continues to hurt them. But to me, this moment looks like respect.

In general, we are a little fuzzy in describing respect and so a little slow to recognize respect when we see it. To me, self-respect is what I see when someone looks at a former self through new eyes and makes the decision to step back into those shoes and add new meaning to old choices. This self respect is not the only agent of healing, but it is the one that makes the difference between temporary relief and a new beginning.

Tell your scar story

If you are reading this, you are probably old enough to have experienced both hurt and healing. You have scars, some visible to other people. One of the most powerful ways to own the part of you that needs to heal is to tell your scar stories. It's easiest to start with an actual physical scar that is relatively easy to talk about. You'll find that it's easy to find listeners for your scar story because all scar stories happen on common ground. We've all crashed through that window, or felt the knife slip. We all know what it is to earn a scar.

If you're shy, you can show your solidarity with the part of you that needs to heal by connecting with other people's scar stories. Some of these you'll find at the movies or the bookstore. Lots of people tell the stories of their scars in big, public ways. Others you will find by encouraging the people around you. People love to talk about their scars. Just open yourself to listening and connecting with the stories. Analysis is probably not helpful if you are working on something major, but paying attention to the story and the fact that it gets told is important. All scar stories are stories of a loss (someone got hurt). All stories are stories of a win, because someone gave shape to something that threatened to overwhelm them. Giving it shape and putting edges around an experience gives a storyteller control over what that experience will mean. Even if the story hurts, the storyteller triumphs.

Paying attention to scar stories will eventually lead you to share a story of your own at a time when you are on common ground with someone who will 'get it.' As you tell the story, you will win, even though the story you tell will be about a different hurt and a different healing than the one that is preoccupying you now. You will win because you will be connecting whatever is on your mind to a previous hurt that created a scar because it healed. When you tell the story, you are the person who was scarred and also the person who is telling the story. You are demonstrating that you can incorporate the experience of being hurt and move beyond it.

Three steps to trusting the ground where healing happens

1. It will be weird to think of creating common ground with yourself until you think about a time when real physical pain seemed to create a barrier between the self in pain and your usual, capable, thinking self. There is a border between your hurting self and your bigger self. That's the ground where healing can happen.

2. It's hard to trust the ground under your feet when you know that you are on the edge of a swamp. That's why healing often happens unconsciously. You don't think about doubting the common ground if you are distracted. You simply stand on it.

3. Acknowledge what you have learned from whatever needs healing. This doesn't mean you have to agree the lesson was worth the price. It does mean noticing that the you that is hurting and the you that will move forward are inevitably connected.

Discovering common ground when solving a problem

There are several ways to think about applying the principle of moving on common ground to the work you do to solve a problem. The first is to know that most of your problems already involve other people and moving on common ground with them will uncover possibilities that satisfy the most requirements with the least possible resistance. The other is to consider the problem as if it were a playing field and notice what parts of that field are already familiar to you. This helps you define how what you already know can point you towards the solution to a new problem. In both of these, you use your experience (as it is stored in your memory and as you interact with others) to generate information about the shared ground most likely to lead to a solution.

The other way to apply this principle to problem-solving is a little more of a stretch. When working with other people, we know that information available through the senses is generally common ground. If two people are standing in the same room with about the same eyesight they will likely see the same things. This is also true, more generally, when you think of a problem as a playing field. The facts about the problem that you can represent in your senses (what you can see, hear and feel) are likely to define common ground more quickly and more accurately than conceptual agreements. It's helpful to describe the problem in these concrete, sensory-defined terms and notice what changes in your state as you approach it this way. You will find that the focus through your senses on the concrete elements of the problem is one of your experiences of being on common ground and it will allow you to feel more present and more connected in helpful ways.

Finding common ground with the uncoachable client

Have you ever encountered a client or team member you thought was uncoachable? It's a frequent issue in coaching, management and sales: the client who cannot be moved. And it's an equally common debate. Are some clients just impossible?

Here is the client who is most likely to seem impossible: she's extremely articulate; she's well-versed in communication and change (including the model you use most often); and she's facing a problem you think might be unsolvable. None of these qualities make her a difficult person. You might like and respect her. It's just hard to out-talk her, and if her talk would set her free, she wouldn't seek coaching. What would you do?

Here's what you could do. You could move on common ground and discover what possibilities emerge. Moving on common ground means that if a client has come to you for coaching, you take it as a shared presupposition that she is coachable and that you are capable of getting a result. That's what you assumed when you set up business as a coach and that's what she assumed in coming to you. Simply acting as though that presupposition were true is the first step. As a coach, you don't get to believe the client in front of you is uncoachable because if you do, you've stepped off common ground.

The next step onto firm common ground is to approach the problem through its representation in the senses. Keep asking "what" and "what else" so that the client leads you onto what you can be sure is common ground because it is represented in common sensory experience. As the client talks and you insist on description that you can imagine, you begin to move more naturally on common ground. Your attention and hers are synchronizing on the sensory details of the problem that needs to be resolved.

The final step is to ask for a step, a sensory-tangible action that the client can take to move towards a solution. It's not your job as a coach to have a solution or even to be able to see the way to a solution. It's your job to focus the client's eyes on the next step on the path to a solution. It's your job to ask "what" and "how" and "where" and "when" so that a next step becomes clear enough in all your senses that you can be sure they are clear in hers.

No one is uncoachable. There's no reason for this process not to work. When you restrict your movement to common ground, you create a focus that reveals new details. It's like crossing a playing field. Knowing where the bumps and holes are will not guarantee that you win the game. But mentally rehearsing the details of the playing field will always yield benefits.

The Six Step Reframe: genuine agreement is a prerequisite

One of the most useful patterns in NLP is known as the six step reframe (Bandler and Grinder, 1979). It is rarely explained in six steps, but the general strategy is immensely helpful in generating good alternatives to behaviours that aren't working for you. It works by finding common ground between the self that doesn't like a behaviour and the self that is doing the behaviour (both of these selves are the real you).

1. Ask yourself why you're doing the thing that isn't working. There's always a positive intention.

2. Tell yourself to generate many, many alternatives to satisfy that positive intention. Trust that you can do this, especially if the alternatives are not coming into conscious awareness.

3. Now choose three behaviours to test. You may or may not know what they are, but just telling yourself that you need to try three new things makes it much more that likely you will generate an alternative when an opportunity exists to try one.

4. Ask yourself if you're actually willing to do these alternative behaviours. There's no sense in walking away from the process until you know that you are prepared to take action.

5. Ask yourself if any part of you objects to any of the new behaviours. This is the part everyone wants to skip. Why not just try something despite objections? We make so many decisions based on a simple majority. But this process requires unanimity.

LIVING YOUR **PURPOSE**

6. If any part of you objects, make friends with that part and choose new behaviours together. And repeat.

It's entirely possible to talk about this pattern as though the important part were a willingness to make decisions based on your unconscious processes. It's true that it requires a commitment to trust your own creativity, and that is a form of moving on the common ground between your conscious mind and unconscious processes. The more important agreement here, however, is the agreement to honour any objections by simply generating new behaviour. Instead of thinking of creativity as so difficult that it requires sacrificing parts of yourself to achieve, you can think of creativity as so natural that you can respect all of yourself (thoughts, beliefs and instincts) when you are problem-solving. This doesn't mean that you will not feel any resistance. We all feel resistance to uncertainty and effort and we make choices to go ahead anyway.

What new choices would occur to you if you stopped overriding your instincts and your doubts? When you think about the problem you do not know how to solve, are you really not able to think of steps you could try to get closer to a solution? It's more likely that you have given up looking because it takes too much effort to run roughshod over some parts of you just to make progress. That's a good instinct. True progress does not come at the expense of part of yourself. It comes when you are willing to do whatever it takes to generate new ideas until you find one that all parts of you are willing to test.

After all, it is a test. You do not know what will work until you try something. While a few problems may be solved in one grand sweep, most of them are solved by one tentative step after another. Each step creates common ground between you and the problem (because it is a concrete action that results in sensory-tangible data). And each step that is taken with the agreement of all parts of you has all parts of you at work on the problem. This makes sense both intuitively and scientifically (which is not the same as saying it has been proven scientifically). If the whole of your brain were to light up while you thought about a problem, it does seem likely that your brain would enjoy the workout and the problem would be closer to being solved.

Three steps to solving problems on common ground

1. As you problem solve, work on ground that is big enough to include all of your resourcefulness. That makes it more likely that you will generate solutions and much more likely that you will generate a solution you like. You will know the solution when you see it (or hear it, or feel it) because your senses are common ground. They link your mind and body, your memories and your perceptions, your speculation and your observation.

2. If your problem involves other people, then a rigorous appreciation of the data available through your senses will be even more important. The more you can translate concepts into sensory-tangible information, the more likely you are to pitch ideas in a form that will stick with the people catching them. You may have shared beliefs and concepts, but you will be more confident that you are on common ground when you agree on how those abstract concepts fit into the world perceived by the senses.

3. When you have been working at a problem unsuccessfully, go back to common ground and work at describing it through your senses. As you do, you will be surprised to discover a new level of detail and a new sense of possibility. It's like the difference between knowing grass is green and really looking at all the different shades of

green in a single blade of grass. Not all the new detail will be useful, but somewhere in the new information you will find the key that unlocks the problem you want to solve.

All influence springs from common ground

If you are reading this book from start to finish, then you will be aware that all the applications involve the process of influence. Healing, problem-solving and goal setting all involve getting yourself and others to behave and think in ways that serve a particular end. In NLP they say that you cannot not communicate; since all communication is a kind of influence, it follows that you are always influencing either your own direction or the thoughts and behaviours of other people.

There is an increasing body of scientific evidence that supports the idea that we are always more aware of our context than we think we are, and that awareness predisposes us to think some things and miss others. In psychology, they do experiments to show that changing mindset changes performance (Dweck, 2006), that changing qualities of the physical setting changes attitudes, and that one good or bad quality can colour our response to unrelated events or people (Kahneman, 2011). As much as this means that we are always influenced by things outside our control and even outside our awareness, it also means that we always have influence, sometimes in ways that are hard for us to predict.

What is not hard to predict is that the influence we have springs from common ground. All the unconscious influences work through our sensory perceptions. If we did not notice change with some part of our neurology, it could not change us. Even unconscious attention is powerful. Conscious attention makes an obvious difference. The people to whom we are paying attention have more influence on us than the people in the background. When someone notices us and reflects back our dreams, our perceptions or our fears, we pay attention to them. It's true that power relationships create a kind of common ground (I am on one end of this club and you will be on the other end), but that common ground only holds within defined conditions. Most of the time, we cannot have enough power to sustain influence through fear (and the price for doing it is very high). It's more effective and more sustainable to influence someone by gaining their attention and moving on the ground you share.

Instructions are a testable form of influence

There are many times when we talk about something that we believe with all our hearts and have no way to know whether or not we have had an influence. This is frequently true of professors and preachers and motivational speakers. Even if they are popular and receive praise for their creativity or passion, it is hard for them to see tangible evidence that they have changed the way someone thinks or acts. There are too many variables and usually too much time between the influence and the results. The more passionate you are about something, the more you need to practice influence in contexts where you can see results. It's the only way to move from having people listen to seeing people change.

In his recent book, *To Sell is Human*, Dan Pink says that 37% of workers give instructions to other people (Chp. 1). Giving instructions is a terrific way to practice influence because you can see the results of your communication. Either people follow the instructions and get the appropriate result or something goes wrong and you know because you do not get the results you expect. In those cases, you often have the chance to modify your instructions and check the results of the changes. If you need to give instructions, you probably have a chance for repetition with difference. In other words, you have a chance to practice mindfully.

Here's what it takes to give great instructions. You have to be so accurate at predicting another person's perceptions and responses that you can begin where they are and lead them step by step through a process that gets real results. The moment you step off common ground, your instructions become fuzzy and your results become unpredictable. Think of a teacher you didn't like and didn't learn from (we all have some in our experience). The odds are that you didn't like the teacher because she or he expected you to do the work of imagining their experience. Teachers who do not imagine the experience of students so they can meet them on common ground do not teach. They give instructions that are rarely followed or remembered. This is not a matter of liking the teacher. It is a matter of neurology. If we can't relate new information to the patterns stored in our brain, the new information simply does not stick. On the other hand, when a new process seems to be built of pieces that are already familiar to us, it is a relatively direct process to reassemble them to get a new result. Teachers accelerate learning by paying attention to the building blocks that are already part of their students' experience.

Think of something you do every day and imagine training someone else to do it the same way you do it and get the same results you get. Before you think about how you would teach them, consider that you now do things without conscious thought that you once had to give your attention. For instance, I once lent my car to one of my son's friends so he could move some musical instruments. I had walked just far enough away from the car so that it would be awkward to go back when I realized the car had not moved. It was only at that moment that I thought all the way back to when I first got that car. There's a barely perceptible collar around the gear stick. To put the car in reverse, you lift the collar and slide the stick to R. If you don't lift the collar, the stick does not slide into reverse. After years, the movement had become an imperceptible part of the way I started the car to back out of my driveway. I had stopped thinking about it and so I hadn't warned the other driver. If he had experience of a car with a similar mechanism, he would also make the movement automatically (possibly without even noticing what he was doing). He did not, and it took him a few frustrating moments (the car loaded with his buddies) before he figured out how to get started.

Practice moving on common ground to give instructions

Here's how you can prepare to give instructions for any task you know how to do well.

1. Write or record a description of what you think you do. You can voice record using your cell phone if you're not a writer, but writing or diagramming is a great way to capture what you've said so you can take a look at what is there and what is missing.

2. When you think the description is complete, ask yourself: what else do I do? Move back to what you do before you start. As you do the task or imagine doing the task, record more information. Your posture and perceptions are as important as the words you say or the analysis you do. Your body often gives you clues about the unconscious processes (the habits) that change the way you do what you do.

3. Now spend some time imagining the person or people you will be instructing. What do they already know and what is new to them? Remember that the unexpected always catches our attention. Something new in the middle of a familiar process can easily throw us off our game whether or not it is actually important. Find a way to highlight the words that might mean something different to them, anything unique in the environment or equipment and

everything that you ever thought "just takes experience" to know. The flip side is that you then need to explore the strengths and skills that the learners possess that persuade you they are capable of following your instructions. If you are unconvinced, they will also be unconvinced. So it is important that you pay attention to what makes it possible that they will learn quickly and well.

4. Have you noticed that we have not yet got to the part where you break the activity into steps analytically? If you jump to this step too quickly, you are not likely to chunk the activity into details and steps that make intuitive sense to the people you are instructing. Logic is less important than experience in creating "steps" for instructions. We do not perceive all information as equal in importance. The information we filter out of awareness may be as important in following instructions as the information we specifically include in awareness. So make sure you are imagining the process as if you were the person or people you are instructing. Notice what they will find surprising, distracting or confusing.

5. One more task before you begin the process of instructing is to design feedback loops so that you will know what is being noticed and understood as you instruct. The key to working on common ground is to notice as soon as you step off of it. If you do not know how you will know you're on common ground, you will leave common ground and hope that the learner follows you into your perception of the task at hand. Sometimes you will be right, but more often that hope results in confused learners and a frustrated instructor. It's much better to assume that it takes willpower to move on common ground and plan to check frequently for understanding and agreement.

Three steps to working on common ground

1. Working on common ground requires calibration. Often people you want to persuade will enjoy your attention and admire the work you are doing. That creates substantial common ground, but not much movement. Movement requires that they agree to listen and then agree to think and act. When you are paying attention to the common ground, you will notice the difference between the two agreements.

2. You're probably familiar with the saying "if you want something done right, do it yourself." That applies to connecting and moving on common ground. If you want to change the way people think, feel or act, then you will be more successful when you make the effort to meet them on common ground.

3. It's tempting to believe that people will do the work to connect with you while you connect to a terrific vision. You will get better results if you step out of your vision enough to monitor what is really changing and what you need to do to move the common ground, even a little.

SET YOURSELF UP FOR SUCCESS

At some point, you will be tired of chasing other people's priorities or you might be tired of encountering everything and everyone as a potential problem. At that moment, you will decide to represent your life in a way that allows you to notice what is helpful, what is right, what is good. You might think of this as setting a goal, or you might think that you are not the kind of person who values goals but you do value knowing what is right. Either way, you will be more likely to be satisfied with your work and your life if you invest some time in imagining a future you would like and value.

You can begin on common ground by noticing what parts of that desirable future are already part of your life. You can look at everyone and everything you encounter as possibly embodying some part of what you value. This alone will change your perspective and your experience. You will go through each day surrounded by potential evidence that what you want and what you value can become real. Every moment becomes a chance to uncover another piece of the puzzle, another clue to discovering a future worth living. Every person becomes a possible example of a strength, a value, a characteristic that would be useful to you in the future you have begun to imagine. The world becomes a place of possibility when you are determined to find in it the seeds of a future worth living.

The common ground between life as you know it and the future you desire is the best place to build for that future. You will uncover it by discovering the common ground between the world perceived by your senses and the world constructed by your imagination. The discipline is to work in the space where mind and body are inextricably linked and the evidence of your feelings (physical and emotional) provides sophisticated intelligence about the ground shared by mind and body. As you focus on clues, you heighten your sensory acuity, and as you heighten your sensory acuity, you widen the ground that is available to both body and mind, both perception and creation. You also heighten your ability to connect with other people, since much of that connection will happen through non-verbal patterns and physical cues.

When you heighten your awareness of your connections to other people, you also automatically begin to consider another common ground: the ground shared by you and the people who will be part of the future you desire. They can only be part of the future you are shaping if it is shaped on ground they occupy with you and they are more likely to occupy that ground when it is either part of their current experience or just one step away from it (since other people are changing and moving as much as you are). Your heightened awareness not only allows you to notice other people as models of characteristics or abilities, it also allows you to notice where you share common values, abilities, interests or expectations. With these in mind, your shaping of the future may shift so that you can continue to move on common ground.

Some of your imagined future is likely to require active agreement and collaboration from these other people. To bring it into being, you will need not only to move on common ground, but to communicate in ways that inspire a shared vision and collaborative action. While it may sometimes feel like you are designing a future within limits set by other people, you will find that accepting those conditions may allow you to be more creative and more productive. Artists in fields from painting to writing to music to performance accept the constraints offered by particular forms because they know those constraints deepen their practice and focus their creativity. In the same way, you will find that shaping a future that meets the needs, interests and perceptions of the people who will share it inspires you to deeper thinking and a focus on actions that will make your ideas tangible to others.

Goals as common ground between the present and the future

Over the years in which I have worked with corporate clients it has become evident to me that the degree to which we can define a goal on shared ground is the degree to which I can be successful in ways that matter to me. When clients take the time to show me who they are and what they want, they get training that feels great and produces great results. The clients who are reluctant to share information or build shared goals still get value from my work, but they are unlikely to be able to realize its potential.

For instance, I worked with a small, high-performing team who were richly collaborative and facing challenging corporate goals. Their manager and their other consultant were both terrific. They absolutely understood the value of being rigorous about taking time to co-create an outcome for the work. When I sat down for two days with the team, we all knew what the real work was. We understood that what we wanted was for every member of the team to make tangible representations of doing the kind of work that would meet their admittedly challenging goals. They came ready to connect with me and with each other. It was not that they were not skeptical. I suspect that they were quite skeptical. It was that they got the results they did because they were able to use their skepticism in the service of tangible, shared goals.

Another group I worked with was exactly the opposite of this one. They were a larger group, some of whom were on the verge of leaving the team (not necessarily of their own accord). Their model was to push hard and trust no one (not even their co-workers). We were asked to work with the group to "introduce NLP" and their leader was too busy to discuss outcomes or even what he understood NLP to be. After literally weeks of proposals and negotiations, we discovered that the leader who had wanted NLP had not actually read the proposals. There is no way to share ground with someone who will neither share information nor consider the information you share. Although you can reach agreements (we did get a contract), you can only move as far as common ground will allow. While we could have used techniques to create the illusion of progress, real progress was limited because there was not enough shared information in the room to support movement. The people in the room in search of new perspectives and techniques took some away with them.

Others missed opportunities because there was not enough common ground to create shared goals.

Build the future on what is non-negotiable

If you are already a person who likes to have goals, you probably have some written down. For you, the future started when you formed those goals and you can grow them now by taking a few minutes to explore three things:

1. When have you experienced having a strength or characteristic that will be useful in the process of achieving this goal? Describe in sensory detail, including what you saw, heard and felt and what someone watching you would have seen, heard and felt.

2. Where in your life now are elements of this future already real? Be precise about the actions, attitudes and beliefs as you experience them now (in yourself or in other people) and elements of your context that will remain constant as you make the changes that lead to your goal.

3. What common ground do you already have with other people who will be part of achieving this goal? Include facts tangible to the senses and information about attitudes, beliefs, strengths and capabilities.

If you are not a person who has found goals helpful, then consider these three questions instead:

1. What's non-negotiable in your context? What is already true in your workplace or home that you would not give up willingly?

2. What's non-negotiable in your behaviours? What is already true in your activities at work or at home that you would not give up willingly?

3. What's non-negotiable in your relationships? Which relationships are important enough that you would not willingly give them up? Within those relationships, what qualities, activities or beliefs are non-negotiable?

Notice that by defining what you value in the life you already have, you are sketching in a sensory-coded version (imagined in terms of what you will see, hear and feel) of a desirable future. It's not as specific as a goal, although it might be more precise in that it includes details that already exist about a future in which you get what you want without sacrificing anything you are not prepared to sacrifice.

Three steps to setting goals on common ground

1. As you will have seen, there is no magic in setting goals and no inescapable failure in living without them. There is, however, an absolute necessity to stay congruent with some aspects of your current identity, relationships and context that you would not willingly sacrifice. Paying attention to what you value is the key to living in a desirable future.

2. If you do choose to set goals, you will want to ensure that they carry you forward on the common ground shared with the characteristics, behaviours, relationships and contexts that you value in your life now.

3. Any version of the future that you wish to shape with one or more other people will come into being more surely and more quickly when it grows from the ground you share.

Patterns Work Like Magic

The world is full of people looking for 'the secret' to something, the magic words, the one key that unlocks power and success. It's hard for most of them to understand that there is no key. People work in complex patterns. When it seems that they are working magic with just one secret, they are actually perceiving patterns instead of pieces. They perceive the pattern and step into it to support or change it and the action seems so confident, so quick and so effective that it is just a little bit magical.

Patterns are hard to wrap our heads around because they contain a paradox. The pattern is defined by the same elements in the same relationships. Yet patterns are also used to create difference within the identity. Everyone who uses the same dress pattern will produce a different dress, and yet all those dresses will also be recognizably the same pattern. Dresses are the simple case. The same is true of patterns of leadership or the patterns we call culture. They are sets of contexts, elements and actions that repeat reliably and allow us to predict what is coming next. They are also building blocks which allow us to take what we know and reinvent it for new purposes or extend it for new range.

The reason patterns are so powerful is that they are the way the equipment works. The human brain does not function primarily in words or elements or keys. Our neurology takes all the activity that happens at one time and wires it into a pattern. Scientists call these patterns neural or cognitive webs. They say 'what fires together wires together' (Edelman, 2005) and what they mean is that our neurology (our minds, our senses, our brains) functions by assuming things are related and then testing the assumption. If the test works, if the same elements reliably occur in the same relationships, then the web strengthens and we form a habit of thought or behaviour. If the test does not work, then we let go of the 'wires' between those elements and free them for new attachments. Since our brain quite literally contains more potential connections than our minds can comprehend, and since it works by comparing, applying and joining whole complexes of connections in a single act, our minds quite often have a hard time explaining what our brains are doing.

Our brains do not prioritize high level abstract reasoning over sensory information in the same way our minds do. They collect information in patterns. Changing one or two elements may be enough to change one of those patterns, and adding one or two elements will exponentially add to the complexity of the pattern even if the information added has little logical value. At some point, the pattern may begin to generate what are called emergent qualities: characteristics possessed by the whole that are not possessed by any of its constituent parts. All of this is actually considerably more complicated than it sounds and it would not be very practical to consider except that the complexity is natural to our brain and our minds are the products that emerge from this complexity. Although it may make your head spin to think about it, this is how you work and you are well-equipped to use this understanding to make changes in your thought, behaviours or circumstances.

LIVING YOUR **PURPOSE**

MAKE THE PATTERN BIGGER THAN THE PAIN

When we hurt, our pain exists in our bodies and our minds. The body responds to a stimulus or circumstance that produces a signal that causes our minds to experience pain. Sometimes our minds experience something that is like physical pain, a mental pain that can cause our brains to send signals throughout our body that come back to us as a perception of physical pain. There are essentially two ways to relieve pain. We can change the physical circumstances causing pain or we can change the perceptions which allow us to notice pain. Ibuprofen, for instance, is an anti-inflammatory drug that reduces the inflammation within the body that results in pain. Acetaminophen, on the other hand, works to reduce the perception of pain without changing its cause. Whether pain is physical or emotional, it can be dealt with by changing conditions or by changing perception. If you are not paying attention to your perception of pain, the pain will disappear for as long as you can maintain the distraction.

Your mind can be distracted but your brain is never distracted. The signals that were creating pain are active even when your conscious awareness is somewhere else. You now have two patterns active at the same time: the pattern that represents the pain and the pattern that represents the distraction. The brain connects these two patterns to form one larger pattern. The distraction does not cancel out the pain, it is added to it (your brain is simultaneously activated by the pain and by the distraction). Adding to the pattern changes the possibilities it contains. In a given moment, you have the experience of pain, the experience of the distraction, and potentially other experiences that could emerge from the combining of the two. You have now created not just two choices, but an unpredictable number of choices. Unless there is a compelling benefit to the perception of pain, you will probably lose track of the pain so that you can pursue another of the choices that emerge.

It's complicated, but it is not hard to understand. We all know what it feels like when our minds get overloaded. We focus on what we can manage and forget whatever does not seem most present or most urgent. Pain often feels most present and most urgent and so crowds out our ability to solve complicated analytical problems (like how to get dinner on the table). After the pain has told its story (you've received whatever medical care is possible), there is no reason for it to remain the most present and urgent thing in your attention. If something else became more present or more urgent, the pain would recede to the back of your mind. It would still be there, but it would not hurt as long as you were thinking of the other thing.

Have you ever woken up and just for a moment forgotten some dreadful loss or hurt? For that moment things are different and you are comfortable. Then the hurt crashes back, and you are once again in pain. These brief moments of freedom are a pattern within a pattern. If you can discover how to make them last, you can imagine pushing the pain into the background indefinitely.

The day the fire alarms went off

We have all had experiences where we ignored some noise (often a fan, sometimes a party next door or construction across the street). At first it was annoying, but gradually we stopped paying attention and the sound seemed to disappear. What if the noise were an alarm? Alarms are designed to be hard to ignore. It's almost painful to listen to them for more than a few minutes. After all, their function is to move you away from them and towards safety.

One January day, a partner and I were co-training a course for coaches. The participants came from a wide radius around Toronto, and it would have been very hard to reassemble them at a different time. About 11:30

a.m., the power went out and the fire alarm started ringing. After a building inspection and a call to security, we knew that there was no fire and there was also no way to turn off the alarms. So we broke for lunch, assuming that by the time we returned we would have light, heat and quiet in which to complete our course.

When we got back, the power was still out and the alarm was still ringing just outside the door where we were training. We were again assured by security that there was a glitch in the system but no danger. We consulted with the group, and they agreed that they would rather keep going than try to reschedule. We had lots of natural light, and we lit some candles to help everyone stay warm. We closed the door and went back to our material. At different points, someone would comment that the fire alarm had finally stopped. My training partner was a police officer with extremely good sensory acuity. He would smile and open the door to demonstrate to us that the alarm was as loud as ever. We had simply stopped noticing it.

I watched the same process happen much more quickly while working with a dear friend who was hospitalized and under the best medical care. In these circumstances, her pain was not conveying any new information: it was an alarm that could safely be ignored. When she was in pain, I began to talk to her in a voice she trusted about a place she loved and sensations she could give attention, first in her body and then in her imagined body. It was a form of trance in which I allowed her to wrap her attention around my voice and the alternate experience it was creating. As she did, I watched her physical body relax. The pain was not an issue as long as my voice supported her in giving her attention to something else.

As mindfulness practitioners will recognize, the key to both examples was the willingness to simply accept the unwanted experience and move on. Any attempt to fight the noise of the alarm or the physical pain would have focused more attention there. The basic pattern was to create a choice compelling enough to be held through the pain until the pain simply became part of the background, acknowledged but unimportant.

A process for managing pain

1. Pain, whether physical or emotional, is a signal that something needs to change in your circumstances to support your well-being. The first step in managing or healing pain is to acknowledge its message. What's wrong that could be made right? What support do you need that you do not have or have not had? Decide that something really does have to change. That something may include elements outside of you but the change will have to begin the only place that you can control, in your own thoughts and actions.

2. Find the edges of the pain. Pain is a pattern that seems to take up all of your attention, and to reside in every part of your mind and possibly all of your body. The truth is that there are edges to the pattern that represents your perception of pain. The only way to find the edges is to imagine that you are not in the pain but observing it. You can do this because your brain is wonderfully diverse and complex and many parts of your brain and your mind are not in the pain but merely connected to it.

    Be aware that your mind does not necessarily have the same edges as your body. You might discover that there are places where the edges of the pain are outside your physical body. That's okay. It's all yours. The key is to allow your attention to repeatedly test the edges of pain/not pain. This takes either help from someone else (as I helped my friend to find her edges) or willpower and often it takes both. If you are experiencing emotional pain, then the edges will be different but the process will be the same. To find the edges, move your awareness outside the pain and look for them.

3. Now that you are confident you have identified the edges, step over them so that you are more thoroughly engaged in something on the not-pain side of the borders. This will often involve becoming involved with someone who is not part of the pain. Our brains are so well-suited to being curious about other people that other real or imagined people can frequently provide a distraction big enough to take us out of our pain. I once knew a small boy who had migraine headaches. As long as he was watching a movie he liked, he was a wizard at stepping outside of the pain and giving all his attention to the movie. When the movie ended, it felt like the headache returned. In fact, the headache had not gone anywhere. He was the one who moved.

Many people have worked through different kinds of physical and emotional pain by offering all of their attention to a project that feels bigger than they are. They work on a cause or a task that allows them to engage fully with people and sometimes with concepts that fill up the whole field of their awareness. This can happen for a long time or a short time. You probably know someone who has handled a painful life event by diving into something hard or complicated. At the time, you might have wondered how that could possibly be a good thing to do. Now you know.

The final phase in this step is to forget the pain so thoroughly that you very seldom remember that it is there at all. Is this always possible? It will not be possible if the pain has information you need about the changing circumstances in which you find yourself. Old pain will flare up if you are in danger of repeating a pattern that has hurt you in the past. However, as long as pain has nothing to which it can stick in your awareness and no good reason for sticking there, you will find it disappears for longer amounts of time. While it is out of your awareness, it is possible that the hurt will heal and one day you may notice that you are no longer working around it because there is no longer a hurt to avoid.

Three steps for changing the pattern of pain

1. When you are managing your own pain or helping someone else to manage their pain, keep in mind that most pain has a point. Once in a while the alarms go off by mistake, and once in a while pain that had a point becomes chronic and loses its connection to conditions within or around you. Most of the time, pain is a signal that something needs to change. Until you accept that message, you will find it hard to escape the pain in any enduring or meaningful way.

2. Pain is a signal, not a motivation. If it were enough to understand that something needs to change, then life would be less complicated than it is. Conscious awareness that something hurts is only one part of a complex pattern. Untangling the pattern and envisioning a more desirable future take patience, persistence and willpower.

3. Willpower is most easily maintained through our connections with other people. When you are serious about hearing what your pain is telling you and making change, you can seek the distraction, support and bigger frames that are offered by the people who want to help, the people who have the skills to help, or the people who are important enough to you that they draw you out of your pain to a place where you can see its edges.

LIVING YOUR **PURPOSE**

Walk Away from the Problem You Want to Solve

Have you heard it said that the best way to solve a problem is to not think about it? The story of the word we use to describe a breakthrough, *Eureka!*, is the story of Archimedes, a mathematician who took a bath and discovered the solution to a problem. The problem was how to measure the volume of a gold crown. The solution was displacement. He noticed the change in the volume of water when he stepped into the bath. The pattern of the two events was connected although solving math problems and taking a bath are very different activities. It is actually because a nice jacuzzi is not associated with work or problem solving that a long warm bath can yield solutions that a day at your desk has failed to yield. Distance and distraction are as important in solving problems as they are in managing pain.

From a distance, you see different pieces of a puzzle in relation to one another. Up close, each appears to be separate and distinct. The way to recognize the pattern is to move your body or your mind far enough away that you can put a frame around the whole of the puzzle. The edges of the frame allow you to see both the edges of the problem and the relationships among the pieces that need to come together. Pattern recognition has often been cited as one of the distinguishing features of genius (Gladwell, 1999). On the one hand, a genius is someone who can see a pattern where other people see unrelated information; on the other hand, a genius is someone who works more quickly and accurately than others because she is manipulating whole patterns and not individual bits of information. To be more like a genius, you need to get far enough away from the problem you want to solve so that you can see all the pieces and see that there is a pattern in them.

The other thing that a genius can do is predict the future more accurately and more quickly than other people. That's because patterns repeat and once you recognize a pattern, it's relatively easy to know what will come next. In fact, all people (not just geniuses) have the equipment to perceive patterns whether or not they exist. We discover or create meaning that allows us to predict what comes next. And when we recognize that our need to find patterns is inherent in our minds and brains, we can use pattern-making more effectively as a tool for solving problems.

Leadership as problem solving

We've all heard of the Socratic method in teaching. It's the method where the teacher leads by asking questions, rather than by giving instructions or making statements. This is also the primary model for many different coaching methods. The coach asks questions until the client uncovers new information about their context or experience that will allow them to act more effectively or to live with more well-being. If your leadership problem is how to engage people thoroughly and direct that engagement towards a particular problem or task, then you might be effective by taking your cue from teachers and coaches. Asking questions is likely to provoke pattern recognition and pattern recognition is likely to lead to answers.

Is it better leadership to give people all of the information or to give them only enough to provoke them to form a pattern? While it seems like complete disclosure is bound to be more efficient, that's not the way human attention works. When we are presented with a complete picture, we often look at the details and miss the pattern they represent. When we are given just part of the pattern, we are often motivated to find the rest of the pattern. We make predictions, test them, and then modify our guesses about how to complete the pattern based on the feedback we get. The human brain is not designed to be a passive consumer of information. The best way to teach is to recognize that the brain wants to discover and test patterns and to only offer enough information so that the outline of the pattern is suggested. Let the details come from the students. The best way to lead is by providing a skeleton for action and allowing others to fill in the details by recognizing what is needed to complete the pattern.

You'll notice that this very book is based on this principle. By giving you the big picture on the beliefs that support NLP techniques, I am suggesting that you begin to explore the details of how these beliefs are embodied in various techniques or how they are embodied in your experience and work. Think of other books you might have read about NLP. Did they try to give you so much of the technique and detail that it was hard to remember and apply? The more terminology creeps into a field, the more doubt newcomers have that they are capable of recognizing and applying the patterns within that field. This becomes a self-fulfilling prophecy. Frustrated by too much detail, they do lose the big picture of how it all comes together to create results. If they looked at the same information with confidence that they could recognize the patterns and use them, newcomers might get results that seemed like genius. Their brains and minds are, after all, uniquely well-suited to recognizing, creating and applying patterns.

A pattern scavenger hunt

Our basic mode for operating in the world is to 'guess and test.' We gather enough information to form a pattern, use the pattern to make predictions, test the results of those predictions and modify the pattern as necessary with new information or new relationships. You can begin to work with this pattern when you notice all the situations in your day that are built on completing thoughts started by other people. If you're a commuter, you might start by noticing the people on the bus or train who are completing the puzzles in their newspaper. You might notice billboards or other ads that depend on the observer to fill in context or a punch line. At work you will notice how often people trail off, leaving someone else to complete their sentence or their thought. You might even notice that walking a different route through the office wakes you up and refreshes your attention so that you are more productive than you expected. Instead of applying a stored pattern, you have woken your brain up to participate in new feedback loops with your environment.

Now pick one person to observe more closely, one person who likes to talk about themselves. Begin to notice that most of their stories are the same story. They are always the hero or the victim; other people help or hurt them in similar ways and amounts; the surprising twist always comes at the same place in the narrative and the ending is always more or less the same. Congratulations. You've noticed a pattern. Because patterns can look different and still share a structure, you will find that everything someone tells you is related through a pattern to their primary reason for talking to you. If they are talking about a relationship problem, all of their stories will tell you something about that relationship. If they are talking about a decision they have to make, all of their stories will be about the strengths, skills or perspectives that will help them make that decision. When people attempt to describe a problem directly, their description is often distorted by mistakes and misjudgments. When they tell a related story, neither they nor you will be distracted by imprecise details. The pattern that emerges in the story will accurately represent the relationships they are perceiving in a particular situation.

Test the patterns you recognize by making predictions about what you expect and observing what actually happens: guess and test. Patterns allow us to react faster and more reliably because we are able to make more reliable predictions about what to expect. If your predictions are wrong, you need to reconsider the pattern to discover missing elements or different meanings. Never assume that a pattern is useful until it proves itself through testing.

Three steps to problem-solving with patterns

1. Step back far enough to see all the pieces of the problem and some clear space around them. This is a metaphor for considering facts, elements, relationships and context from a point of view that is disengaged. If you internalize the problem, you will not have the perspective you need for pattern recognition.

2. Allow yourself to tell stories about the relationships you notice between different elements of a problem. You will know that you are maintaining the right attitude toward pattern recognition when it is easy for you to move from noticing a pattern to testing it.

3. Patterns lead to solutions because they allow fast, accurate predictions about what to expect in a given situation. Use any pattern you think you notice to generate a prediction and then test the validity of that prediction. If it works, use it to build a solution. If it doesn't work, step back and repeat the process as often as necessary.

PATTERN RECOGNITION IS THE KEY TO INFLUENCE

When people recognize patterns in data or concepts, we call them geniuses. When people recognize and shape patterns in situations, we call them innovators. And when people recognize and change patterns in other people, we call that teaching, selling, coaching, leading or manipulating. Perhaps it is natural that the form of pattern recognition that has the most impact on us is also the hardest to see clearly. Whether we are grateful for influence or furious about it, influence always means that someone has seen a pattern in us and either slipped into that pattern to leverage it or slipped a new element into that pattern to provoke change in an attitude or behaviour.

The process happens in three stages:

1. We make a connection with someone through context, rapport and attention. For the most precise influence, all three elements have to support the connection.

2. We recognize patterns in other people in the same way we recognize them anywhere else. We study the information accessible to us and then we allow ourselves to be distracted until a pattern comes into our awareness. This is most likely when we are in a state of relaxed responsiveness where we have heightened awareness of our surroundings (including other people) without the apprehension that often accompanies that kind of sensory acuity.

3. Once you recognize a pattern, you have the ability to either support it or change it. Either choice has repercussions for the person you influence and often for you, too. Many of these will be outside your awareness much less your control. Best practice is to work with small changes and test the responses.

You may be aware of research done by Kevin Dutton and published in his book, *Split-Second Persuasion: The Ancient Art and New Science of Changing Minds (2011)*. Dutton argues that psychopaths and sociopaths are very good at persuasion. Part of the reason for this is that they are always in that state of relaxed, focused detachment that improves pattern recognition. This is true whether they are the kind of sociopaths who end up in jail or the kind that end up in the C-suite. The price of emulating them is spelled out in *The Game* by Neil Strauss (2005). The book explores the subculture of pickup artists and the price they pay emotionally when their strategies and score-keeping distort both their focus and their ability to make normal human connections.

Pattern recognition within human connections is inevitable. You can no more avoid it than you could avoid suddenly remembering you left the door unlocked or suddenly knowing the solution to a problem you had been working on for months. Once you have recognized a pattern, it also becomes available for application whether or not you choose to be consciously aware of it. It's the way the mind/brain/body equipment works. Being able to learn from one another's experiences is an evolutionary advantage and is as natural as eating or sleeping. Forcing pattern recognition in the way that pickup artists or other manipulators do abuses the natural function. It overloads the conscious mind with patterns and produces unintended consequences (primarily in the influencer). A better approach is to focus on making respectful connections and testing frequently for impact.

Who taught you to be nervous?

People get nervous about different things. Some people get nervous about public speaking or taking tests or going too fast or going too slow. Almost everyone gets nervous about something. Have you ever wondered why? It's rare for a two-year-old to be nervous. They get angry or stressed or overstimulated but they don't get nervous. At some point, either their bodies change to support the state of nervousness or they learn to be nervous. No one intentionally teaches children to be nervous. Somehow, we all learn it anyway. When we do, we pick up the pattern so smoothly that it feels entirely natural. We never believe we are making ourselves nervous. We think that something outside us is producing the effect.

The truth is that the outside stimulus has this effect because you have learned a pattern that connects that stimulus to changes within your body and perceptions. It took many years of NLP training and observation (and more than a little intervention from a skilled NLP trainer) to convince me that I didn't have to be nervous in a car. I thought that nervousness was a sensible apprehension that reminded me to be careful in a dangerous situation. It might be, but my nervousness was also a learned behaviour. When I chose to connect with someone who was never nervous in a car, I began to allow that pattern to change.

What would be different if you recognized your nervousness as a pattern you had picked up from someone else? Would you keep it because it has some benefits to you now, or would you give it back?

Testing for influence

Influence is a loop where something that begins as an intention in your mind results in a change in someone else's behaviour or state. Because both state and intention are fluid in you and in the person you are influencing, it is more useful to notice when behaviour you wanted to elicit appears than it is to try to be certain that you were the cause of that behaviour. The signals you are sending and receiving through your sensory awareness of movement, expression, allusion and patterns are far more subtle and far faster than your ability to track an interaction consciously. If you're not sure this is true, just remember the last time someone claimed you made them do something. You probably instantly rejected the claim and gave a list of completely different factors that influenced their behaviour. That doesn't mean you were right and the other person was wrong. It means you were both describing a situation in which many elements were outside your ability to notice or analyze.

It is more helpful to practice noticing the influence you would like to have and then noticing when you see the behaviour or state you wanted to elicit. Begin with fairly simple, overt behaviours. Have you ever wished someone else would sit up straight or stop fidgeting? Assume that you have the power to intervene, and that power might be more straightforward than you think. Often it's enough to relax as you notice the behaviour you don't like and then introduce in your own body the behaviour or state that you would like to see instead. For instance, as you relax and focus on someone fidgeting, you are likely to move in ways that feel comfortable to you. You may not match the fidgeting exactly, but you are likely to echo it in some part of your body or rhythm. When you feel that a connection has formed, simply quiet the part of you that is moving. Now watch what happens. It's likely the fidgeting will stop.

People are also extraordinarily sensitive to the patterns formed by combining words and movement. If you ask them a question with words, watch their hands. They will often signal the answer before they articulate it. You can also test this the other way around. If you'd like someone to lower their voice (either volume or pitch), spend a moment tracking it with your hand. As the voice goes up (volume or pitch), so does your hand. It may feel awkward to do it intentionally but it is actually something that happens frequently enough to be inconspicuous to the speaker (who is, after all, occupied with their own words and thoughts). After a moment or two, relax and lower your hand. Pay attention to the drop in their voice that follows. If the connection is solid, the changes will be almost simultaneous. It may be hard to feel sure you introduced the change but it should not be hard to notice that something changed in precisely the way you wanted it to change.

Three steps to recognizing the patterns of your own influence

1. Influence is the natural result of patterns that form between two or more people. It often happens outside the awareness of one or both parties.

2. Influence means that your thought is completed in another's state or action. Practice noticing when this seems to happen without paying attention to the mechanism by which it happens.

3. When someone else steps into your pattern, your pattern changes. You will notice that something feels awkward or unfamiliar although you may not be sure why. Trust your instinct. Relax so that your own pattern recognition improves and decide whether or not to accept the change. It's your pattern, after all.

FIND THE PATTERN AROUND YOUR NEXT BIG DECISION

There are many kinds of goals. The one that we have been considering in this book is the one you create, often with no idea of how you will make it real. Another kind of goal is the choice you make when an opportunity lands in front of you. Will you go or will you stay? There is never enough information. Life doesn't come with control groups to test the options. Whatever you choose will set your direction. That's what makes a choice a kind of goal.

Step back for a moment and tell yourself the story of a time you had a choice to make. You can write it out or you can just work through it mentally, but tell the story as you would tell it to a friend. The great thing about telling a story to a friend is that we worry less about our style and storytelling ability and more about connecting in a positive way with someone so that both people are supported or encouraged or enriched.

LIVING YOUR **PURPOSE**

If you wanted your friend to know what it was like for you to make that choice and how you knew what to do, where would your story start? Where would it finish? You could start with the situation that forced you to choose, or you could start before that. You could end with the moment of decision or you could carry on to its consequences. As we tell ourselves the stories of our lives, the beginning and ending of the stories tend to be invisible. They feel natural or automatic. We start where we start and we finish when we're done. It's only by stepping back and looking at the story in the context of our whole life that we realize we made choices about where to start and where to end. Those choices changed the meanings in the story. Those choices changed the pattern.

Sometimes it seems to me that the whole of my work in NLP is asking questions that make a story longer or shorter, deeper or wider or taller. The facts are the facts are the facts. The frames change and that changes the patterns we see. The patterns become our predictions of what we will do next and what results we will get. Whatever we see in front of us becomes a prophecy. When we pay attention to something, we filter the information available to us to support our focus. The pattern that is apparent only changes, our predictions for the future only change, when we make the context bigger or smaller. When you tell the story of an event, you could begin with an ancestor three generations back and continue to the present moment. You could start with the moment before a choice and end with the first result or the most important result. The start and finish change where the middle is and what it holds. They change whether it's a story of triumph or heartbreak or coming home. When I work with the frame of someone's story, they see the facts in new ways. Even if they go back to their first choice, they know it is a choice, not an inevitable reality.

When you tell the story of your choice, the story becomes a pattern that you will apply to new choices unless you make an effort to change it. When you consider the decision you need to make, you will notice that there is a pattern in the story you tell about the decision and that pattern will likely point to one choice or the other. Before you decide, step back and look at the patterns around the decision, the stories that are bigger or longer than the decision itself. The bigger patterns will give you new perspective on what you are choosing and how it moves you in a direction you will value.

The problem of living beyond your patterns

The problem with being fifty in the first part of the current century is that we are no longer sure what patterns apply to us or where we are in the pattern we thought we were living. This has been true for every client I have worked with who feels passionate and energetic and curious and who is living in corporate and social patterns that expect people over fifty to be described by words like mature or seasoned or retired. These are accomplished, successful people who have no model for what they want to be next. They have raised families, developed careers and explored the world through travel or activities. Some of them have been financially successful so that income is no longer a primary concern. Others of them are still very engaged in earning a living. Either way, their options are limited. They knew what they wanted to be when they grew up, and now they've been there and done that. Where are the patterns that will tell them how to make choices now?

Fifty is not the new thirty. At thirty, most people still have a life story about finding a place in the world through work and relationships. Even when thirty was 'old,' thirty came with a pattern and a menu of choices. Fifty somethings are now looking ahead at quite possibly thirty or forty years of health. The stories they have inherited do not fit either their circumstances or their goals. Of course a few will find their way to leadership positions in a fairly well-established pattern, but most people are simply frustrated and confused. How did such smart people end up with such unsatisfying options?

The answer is that we all live in patterns that are largely outside of our awareness and we focus our conscious efforts on immediate goals which are supported by those patterns. When those patterns no longer generate goals automatically, it's time for new patterns. Changing the bigger patterns in your life takes both willpower and curiosity. It means systematically retrieving your own story and making it bigger by adding new elements to the existing patterns. Many people find this process both difficult and fascinating. They retrieve the ability to be curious, engaged and energetic that was natural to youth and make it a deliberate choice. Choosing something that was once unconscious always feels odd. It's like thinking about how you ride while you are on the bicycle. Just noticing what you are doing can throw you off balance for a time. But once you achieve the ability to think and stay moving, you have achieved a new level of mastery and more predictable results.

A whole generation now seems to be looking for ways to forge a longer pattern into which they can fit new goals. Others may face the same kind of dilemma when they confront a health issue or change in circumstances that changes the pattern in which they expected to live. The change first prompts an awareness that there was a pattern and that awareness is awkward and unfamiliar. Then there is a period when they reorganize the pattern or add to it to accommodate the new circumstance. Finally, if they are deliberate about shaping their own story, they will relax into a focus within the bigger pattern and life will become familiar again.

Stretch the pattern around your goals

Begin with a story that you know well. It could be a favourite book or movie, the history of your favourite sports team or a family story. As you think about this story, ask yourself how it could be bigger. Would you tell more about the history or social background, or would you go forward in time and tell more about what comes after the story ends? Just choose the easiest way to expand the scope of the story. You could choose to become more detailed, cover more time, or include more people or spaces (connect it to historical events, for instance). As you work with the story, you will discover that it's a natural process. As a kid, you probably expanded the stories you loved without realizing that's what you were doing.

Now you have a pattern for sketching out a pattern. Try again, but this time make your own story bigger. You might include more family members or family history, or extend your personal story to connect with your community, nation or race. You might connect your real life to your imagined life and include the people and places who have influenced you. You might think of your physical reality and extend your story by connecting to the physical world in new ways. Whatever you do, your story will now contain exponentially more information and more relationships than it did before.

Now step away from the new story. Let it settle. Find ways to distract yourself into a state of relaxed responsiveness. Maybe you'll be like Archimedes and take a nice warm bath or maybe you'd rather go dancing. Some people find it easier to achieve relaxed focus when they are on their own and others think better with company. Remember that patterns are best discovered when you are not thinking about them. That's why we so often tell people, "you'll know it when you see it." We mean that if you stop searching and analyzing, you'll be able to get far enough away from a pattern to recognize it.

LIVING YOUR **PURPOSE**

Notice that you have shaped a story that satisfies you out of the elements that life has given you. You haven't wished away any of your experience or any difficult choices but you may have found new meaning or new value in them. From this point, you can go back to that difficult decision you were facing and ask yourself which choice fits better in this pattern. If you're happy, make that choice. If you're not happy, decide whether you would rather change the choice or change the pattern.

Three steps to using bigger life patterns to discover your goals

1. The stories you tell both reflect and determine the patterns in which you are living.

2. When a pattern no longer provides satisfying choices, it's time to make it bigger by extending one or more dimensions.

3. Once you've extended a pattern, return to a state of relaxed responsiveness before noticing patterns to apply and new choices to make.

LIVING ON PURPOSE

Does it seem obvious to you that it is better to have goals than to not have goals? If you look around, you will find that most people have personal short-term goals (planning a trip or a purchase, for instance) and only a vague sense of what they want beyond that. Their jobs may be largely based on working towards or around the goals that other people set for them. In their personal lives, they may be playing out the roles expected of them. They know what social benchmarks are there to reach and they may set goals so that they reach expectations or compete successfully with those around them. Mostly they just go with the flow.

In some ways, living without goals sounds very peaceful, a way to accept without question what life offers. The truth is that for most people, living without goals places them in quite a frightening world. They spend their days looking for trouble and their nights having trouble sleeping. As they look around them, their conscious awareness does what it has evolved to do: it looks for problems and dangers. It filters out awareness of the good things around them because good things are not likely to pose a threat to the one goal which all living beings share, the goal to stay alive.

The consequence of being satisfied with what you have is often that you live in a world full of threats to that satisfaction.

The only way to change the way your attention filters your experience is to set a compelling goal. This gives your attention another filter or set of filters. It can search for opportunities as well as threats. Without a goal, there is no way to tell whether change is good or bad. The default in our attention is set to assume that change is dangerous. We override that default when we have a clear representation of what we want. Now attention looks for connections between our experience and the experience we want to have.

This means that any goal is better than no goal. Our experience of the world is the experience of what we notice and any goal opens us to the possibility that the world holds both threats to our survival and opportunities to make our lives more satisfying. Since people naturally work in patterns, new goals must connect to existing patterns. You can attach a new goal to the pattern that is top-of-mind at the moment, but that will leave you more or less at the mercy of situations as they arise. A better way is to have a pattern that is broad enough and continuous enough that you can attach new goals to it and have confidence that achieving those goals will allow you to build more satisfaction.

Think of a purpose as a set of goals comprehensive enough to ensure that wherever you are, whatever you are doing, the possibility exists that you will find outside yourself things that carry you forward and offer hope of increased satisfaction. If your purpose involves other people, you immediately enrich all your relationships with the possibility that other people will offer you what you need to satisfy some aspect of your purpose. Just as assuming that resources are there allows you to find resourceful people wherever you go, having a purpose allows you to notice that there are often people or resources available to help you satisfy that purpose. The world feels like a safer, more balanced, and more satisfying place.

Is healing a default or a choice?

Biologically, we share with other creatures a common purpose: the imperative to stay alive. It's not absolute: sometimes people will give up their lives in the service of a purpose they believe is worth the sacrifice. But most of the time, our bodies and unconscious processes work to keep us alive. We get hungry and thirsty and cold to remind us our bodies need food and water and shelter. We do not need to make a conscious decision for healing to occur when our bodies are sick or injured. Our bodies work to keep us alive.

It is true, however, that even physical pain sometimes requires a conscious intention to heal or to heal more quickly or effectively. Physical therapy works because we seek therapy and do the exercises assigned to us to build the strength we need to move comfortably. Many conditions require that we intervene in natural processes (with medicine or surgery) so that we can heal. When conscious intention works with our natural healing processes, we become better more often in more situations with more efficiency. It's not enough to wait to heal. We also have to set a goal to heal.

The same thing is true emotionally. It is said that 'time heals all wounds' but most of us have experiences that we have allowed to scar over but not to stop hurting. We have memories that hurt us, and those memories can influence us even when we are not conscious of them. We remember betrayal or failure and set filters to look for warning signs in the world around us, even when the betrayal or failure happened in a different time, in a different part of our lives. Natural healing leaves scars and natural emotional healing leaves us in a less-than-friendly world. If we want signs that the world can support us emotionally or intellectually as well as it does physically, we require a purpose big enough so that we scan our experience for signs this is true. Often this starts by deciding to look for what we need to heal whatever is still causing us pain or changing our perceptions in ways that draw us back into a pattern that caused pain.

Who does the healing?

One of the most famous patterns in NLP is called the fast phobia cure. It is a relatively simple cognitive re-patterning so that a stimulus stops causing irrational fear. The idea is this: in a phobia, it is not the thing itself that causes pain but the individual's response to the thing. If the individual can be helped to respond differently, there is no phobia. We say that it has been cured. Since a phobia is an irrational fear, there can be no harm in getting rid of it.

The mind is not like the body. The mind is continuous with the body as one integrated system, but it's not made of the same stuff. When a body heals, we can study the process and we know what is different at the end. When the mind heals, we cannot see the traces. We have to make a decision about what to believe. Did the mind heal itself (possibly with assistance)? Or did someone else heal the mind? Who is the active agent of healing?

Our answer to the question is based on the first two principles at the heart of NLP. If the mind and body are a continuous system and everyone has the resources they need to live a more satisfying life, then everyone has what they need to heal a hurt that affects both the mind and the body. Other people can support the goal of healing, but they cannot set that goal for you and they cannot carry it out. If you need to heal, then you need to do the healing.

Setting a goal to heal

When I was just beginning in NLP, someone told me that I was going to cure their migraines. At the time, I had no concept of how that could be true. I was not sure I believed anyone could make migraines go away and I was sure that I had no skills to do such a thing. Later, I came to understand that just setting the goal to end the migraines would be powerful. Attaching it to someone you saw often so that all positive interactions could be applied to the goal of curing migraines was a very elegant way to create both the detachment to see opportunity and the willpower to use it. Within a year or two of making the absurd statement that I could cure migraines, this person's migraines had stopped.

It's easy to create conditions that work with someone who has a strong intention to feel better and an openness to finding what he or she needs. As my friend with the migraine demonstrated, it is possible to heal yourself by anchoring your goals and expectations to someone you trust to demonstrate useful patterns and make positive suggestions. They do not have to be deliberately intervening in your goal. It is your attention that is doing the heavy lifting. The most important part of any healing is the determination to uncover the resources that will allow you to heal.

Could you heal your own phobias?

We all recognize that sometimes we need other people to help us reach our goals. Personally, I am not an electrician, a plumber or a surgeon. When I have a goal that requires any of these forms of expertise, I carry out my intention by making use of external resources. I hire experts in their fields. I only need to be expert at identifying what I need and who can help.

People who do not have phobias do not understand that an irrational fear can be crippling. If your phobia is more of the type that makes you squeal when a mouse runs across the kitchen floor, it's possible that you can change that on your own. If your phobia is one of those that paralyzes you with fear, one that seriously impacts your ability to achieve your goals, then you already know that you cannot tackle it without outside assistance. You need someone else to hold the belief that you have the resources to deal with this because in the grip of the phobia, you cannot hold that belief yourself.

When I work with other people's phobias, I am able to hold my purpose and my belief that they have the resources to heal. I am able to do this because this is the price of admission to do the work. If, for a moment, I give up my belief that this person can deal with this problem, I become useless. My purpose allows me to hold the requisite belief. The certainty that the person has what they need to heal guides my ability to work gently around the edges until I see that they are ready to do the big work. I could not work on my own phobias this way. For myself, I would hope that the work at the edges was enough because the big fear would rob me of the beliefs necessary to do the work. If you think this would not be true of you, you are not dealing with this kind of phobia or trauma. The way irrational fear or memory works on the inside is quite different than the way they look from the outside. No one can simultaneously be terrified and be convinced that the terror can be overcome.

Here's how the NLP phobia cure works. The practitioner helps the client access resources. They remember times of strength or happiness and anchor them with a touch or an object. When the client is easily able to access the resources, the coach asks them to briefly enter into a memory of the phobia and anchors that. In NLP, the assumption is that people know their phobias well and need to spend only enough time thinking about them to stabilize their representation.

With both resources and phobia anchored, the change process begins. It is so hard to dissociate from a phobia or trauma that the process begins with a double dissociation. The client is asked to see himself in a movie theatre, waiting for the movie to start. He imagines standing in the projection booth or another protected space at the back of the theatre, watching himself sitting next to the practitioner. When the dissociation seems stable, the practitioner asks that the client notice the person sitting in the movie theatre is holding a black and white photo of the first time he experienced the phobia.

The practitioner reminds the client that he can use (in NLP, the term is 'fire') his resource anchor at any time that he feels uncomfortable. The coach can also fire the anchor at any time she senses that the client needs more resources. After this reminder, the client is instructed to watch himself throw the picture up towards the screen, so that it fills the screen. The client is now watching himself watch a movie of the first time he experienced the phobia or trauma. As he watches, he fires the resource anchor to give him the strength to watch without being drawn into the trauma or phobia. The practitioner then encourages the client to manipulate the movie, running it backwards and forwards, adding funny music, or changing the speed or the colours. They play the movie again and again until the client can play the movie without needing to access the additional resources.

When the movie can be played comfortably, the client is told to move his awareness back into the person sitting in the movie theatre and holding a black and white photograph. He then invites the self from the photograph to come out of the photo so the client can assure him that he will never have to experience the trauma again. It's finished. The client then pulls the dissociated younger self into himself, so that the double reintegration is complete.

After the process, the practitioner can fire the resource anchor and check that the fear associated with it has gone. When you think about this process, you will notice many times where it would be easy for the client to be drawn back into the experience of the phobia if it were not for the stability and purposefulness of the practitioner. The practitioner does not 'heal' the phobia, but she does make healing possible by keeping the phobic state at a distance long enough for the client to learn that he can control his inner representation of the experience which caused the fear in the first place.

You could use straightforward cognitive behavioural therapy to desensitize yourself to some mild phobias. If you don't like spiders, you could practice looking at pictures of spiders, playing with spider toys, visiting spiders in museums, or deliberately encountering live spiders until the fear diminished. This would be unpleasant but probably not unbearable, and you would accomplish the goal of learning to control the way you represented spiders internally so that they no longer caused irrational, disproportionate fear. But even with this milder case, you would be more likely to persevere through the steps if you were accountable to a support person or professional.

Three steps to setting a goal to heal

1. The next time you notice that you are in pain, whether that pain is physical or emotional, begin by taking a breath and telling yourself that you intend to feel better and to heal the cause of the pain. No

one can do this for you, and without this, most interventions will be of limited value.

2. Once you have a goal, become aware of the people and circumstances around you that will support healing. You might find a practitioner to help you with physical pain or emotional pain. You might find consultants or professionals to help you with the "pain" you feel when frustrated at work.

3. Curing pain often involves facing that pain and using willpower to move towards the goal of eliminating it and dealing with its source. Healing is an unconscious process, but it is driven by conscious determination and expert help.

Does purpose trump problem?

On the one hand, any problem you experience is a problem because it stands between you and a goal or a desired direction. On the other, you probably know many people who are so caught up in problems that they forget what they wanted in the first place. All we need is a sketchy sense of what other people want from us and a desire to be comfortable and life can seem to present an infinite string of obstacles to doing what is necessary to maintain peace. Some problems are hard to solve and others just lead to new problems. This is so often the case that some people will describe their days as a string of problems that they solve or confront. That's life, they might say.

From another point of view, problems are only really problems when you are afraid you lack the ability or the resources to solve them. Most learning occurs when people take on problems that are just outside the reach of their conscious abilities and work until they gain either a solution or at least a new understanding of the problem. If your purpose is to learn and grow, you can satisfy that purpose even when you are not sure you are closer to resolving the problem. If your purpose requires a solution, then your situation is quite different.

The way to decide what you need to solve a problem is often to step back and take another look at the goal or purpose that is being blocked by this problem. A clear, compelling vision of a desired future will often lead to either a solution or a work-around for a problem that seemed insurmountable.

How does this work exactly? The more you focus on a problem, the more you filter information until it seems like everything in your awareness is part of the problem. When you step back and look instead at the purpose that would be served by a solution, you begin to see that the world includes more possibilities than you thought it did. You filter for information related to the purpose and that allows you to reframe the problem, to see the problem within the bigger frame of the purpose and whatever in your environment or relationships might support your progress towards that purpose.

That's why possibility thinking ultimately trumps problem thinking. The possibilities are defined with reference to a purpose and the problem is just a subset of those possibilities. The possibility frame depends on the purpose to exist. On the one hand, tight problem frames are a problem because they don't let enough information into your consciousness. On the other hand, without some kind of frame there is too much information to process and so possibilities may exist around you without coming into awareness. Purpose thinking creates a frame in which possibilities can exist within and around the problem and attention can settle, process and create.

LIVING YOUR **PURPOSE**

LET PURPOSE DRIVE YOUR PROCESS

About two years ago, I ran up against a problem I had been considering for several years. The problem was how to train trainers to competency within a relatively short time and without a large group for them to "practice" on. This is a problem that confronts anyone who wants to train people to lead groups. If the goal is to be able to run a group of twenty, you would need people who were willing to be guinea pigs nineteen times for every one time they practiced leading the group. That's not an efficient use of time or patience.

On the other hand, an audience or class deserve fully competent people at the front of the room, and competence takes practice. Without knowing exactly how it would be possible to use the skills of NLP to accelerate the skill development of NLP trainers, I gathered a small group of trusted trainees and we talked at length about how to break the skills necessary to run an NLP Practitioner training into smaller units for practice (in NLP it is called chunking down). As we did, we built a compelling sense of purpose. We were all on the same page about how the skills would look, sound and feel when they were working and we were all committed to building the skills the organization needed. I put together training days built on specific competencies including those that are hardest to practice: an awareness of time and timing; the ability to use resistance to build learning; and the ability to check in with oneself and maintain an optimal state through long days, disruptions and creative tension.

A little over a year later, I graduated my first trainers, amazed at how far we had come as a team and how far they had progressed individually. We all brought different perspectives and strengths to the table, and we had learned to be curious (not stressed) about how those differences could yield shared results. The flexibility in NLP processes allowed us to use individual strengths to frame and explain and we had used the consistency of our shared purpose to keep us on track and create a unified approach to the material. There was only one key to the success (although many skills and layers). That key was to 'guess and test.' We guessed how best to approach the challenges and then checked in, over and over again, with whether we were still making progress on our purpose. Whenever we hit a snag, the first reaction was not to analyze a problem. It was to return to the purpose and check on how clear we were on what we wanted.

Roundabouts can be faster than traffic lights

Going straight at a problem is often not the most elegant way to solve it. In many parts of the world they use roundabouts instead of traffic lights at busy intersections. Sometimes, it seems, you can get where you want to go more quickly if you work around an obstacle instead of going straight at it.

This is certainly true of solving a problem that is standing between you and a clear purpose. One way to make progress is to simply ignore the problem. Move to one side so that you can see around it, and take a closer look at what you want. If this sounds too easy to you, try it. You'll find that often the problem that has you stuck has also captivated your attention. If you ask yourself, "what do I want?" the answer is likely to be "I want a solution to this problem." But problems are never the point in and of themselves. They are problems in relation to a goal or purpose. If you can't immediately identify what that purpose is, ask yourself, "When I solve the problem, what will that get me?" Repeat the question until the answer is something that rings true with you, something you know is aligned with your purpose even if you do not have a clearly worded analysis of how this is true.

Here's how the process works. My problem at this moment is that I have the beginning of a headache. When I ask myself, "if I solve this problem, what does that get me?" the answer is that I can keep writing. Then I ask "what does writing get you?" The answer to that might take me through business development, but probably leads me to some identity-level statements about being someone who understands and connects by writing. I write and I am a writer. I am also a teacher and the writing both informs and disseminates my teaching. Now ask yourself: what do you think happened to the headache while I was focused on writing as essential to the way I want to relate in the world? That's right. While I was focused on my purpose, my problem disappeared from my awareness. As I check back in, the problem is still there, but it is no longer stopping me.

Three steps to connecting with your purpose

1. If you have to solve your problem to connect with your purpose, you might be doomed. A problem that is worth the name has you stuck. It threatens to take up all of your attention. The solution you are looking for is probably not in the picture you see when the problem fills your inner movie screen. The resources you need are likely to be outside the edges of that picture.

2. Looking at your purpose draws your eyes away from the fascination of the problem and makes it much more likely you will notice something at the edges of the screen that will contribute to finding a solution.

3. To solve a problem, look at your purpose and let the problem rest in your blind spot. If the problem moves or changes you will notice. If it stays still, you can look around it to find what you need.

Having a purpose is a giant step towards influence

If you found it difficult to think about your purpose or to imagine how a particular goal would serve that purpose, you now understand that most of the people around you are at least a little fuzzy about what they want. They may be searching for an answer, testing possibilities, or just going with the flow in the hope that something will click for them. In this state of indecision, it will seem possible that the direction you offer them is a good one. As long as you offer a congruent sense of direction, they are likely to accept that direction until something changes in them or in the situation.

As you look back at your life, you can recall times when someone with a clear sense of what was right influenced you to do or think something you would not otherwise have done or thought. Later, you might have wondered what you were thinking. Outside your conscious awareness, you were thinking something like this: I am not clear what I want or what to do. This person is very clear. Maybe if I try this, I will become clear too. This is, after all, one of the basic patterns our minds run (in the background) to allow us to learn from other people's experience. It may have turned out that their purpose was not actually in line with your satisfaction or well-being but you would have needed more clarity on your purpose to be able to judge this without taking a step or two in their direction.

When you are absolutely clear, you become a kind of beacon for people who are living in a fog. They are attracted to your congruence and your purpose. Even if your ideas are not immediately appealing, the possibility that those ideas will generate clarity and direction is appealing. You may imagine that committing to one position makes it less likely that others will be influenced by you. This presupposes that everyone else also has a clear direction. The reality is that when you commit to a purpose, some people will be outside your influence because they also have a clear purpose that is not in line with yours. These people may respect you as purposeful people who disagree. And many others will step onto common ground with you in the hopes that what you want will turn out to be what they want too.

How purpose sets the frame for change

Have you had to push someone to do something that scares them? It is often a part of my work. As a teacher, as a coach, and sometimes as a business partner, I stand with someone at the edge and push a little until they step over it. Whether the edge is the fear of public speaking, the fear of being over their heads, or the fear that what they have mastered will not be enough, it is my work to get them past it and to allow them to see the world from the other side of the edge.

Sometimes I train people to make presentations. I know they are scared. Speaking in public is a fear as pervasive as the fear of snakes or spiders. The anticipation leading up to speaking, and sometimes the act of speaking, can be physically uncomfortable and emotionally challenging. Part of training speakers is managing fear.

Sometimes I train people to be coaches. One of my guiding beliefs is that anyone who offers one-to-one coaching will sometimes be asked to navigate dangerous and unfamiliar waters. People are surprising in ways they cannot even predict themselves. Doing intense coaching work means recovering parts of them they may have lost (sometimes for quite good reasons). It means that they will be resistant or confrontational or, most terrifying of all, utterly trusting. Good coaches are good because they can work on the edge of their own competence while taking their clients to the edges they need to visit.

As a business partner, my role has often been to communicate the particular strengths of the people with whom I am working. This sounds like a gift, until you live it and understand that it is very hard to look clearly at your own strengths. It's hard to realize that one of the functions of putting something into words is to make us take a clearer look at it. No matter how gentle or generous the words, having someone point to something you have not recognized in yourself is unnerving. It implies that you do not know yourself as well as you might like. And it challenges many assumptions you may have about what you could be doing.

The only way I can do the work I do is to grow my purpose so that it is strong enough to encompass all the uncertainty. I need to be able to look at students, clients and partners and be absolutely sure that they can make it across the edge and like what they see from the other side. I need to know they have the strengths and resources they need, especially when they are not sure. My purpose requires that I hold this belief so that others can discover that they are more than they think they are. It's not a guarantee that they will be everything they want to be, but it is the leverage I need to get them to find out what is possible.

If you're not sure how this works, connect with a memory of someone who believed you could do something that scared you. It doesn't have to be someone you liked or someone who supported you. It could be the boss who made you do something you did not want to do. As you access that memory, you will discover how powerful that belief was, how much you were pushed or pulled or changed because someone else held a purpose that included your ability to do something new. Certainty is powerful and we only find certainty in the moments when we know what is right, what needs to happen, what our purpose is in this place and this moment. It doesn't always play out as noble and high-minded. Sometimes it just means knowing that you can reach a target your team has never reached before. Sometimes you are just the kid climbing onto the counter to reach the cookie jar.

Practice finding solid ground

How can you get better at building a clear enough purpose to influence others to change their minds or behaviours? You have to start within a particular frame. Begin by deciding where you want to notice change or progress. Do you want to make a difference in a personal relationship or a work situation? Which person or group, specifically, do you want to influence? Pick just one. It will help to write a few sentences describing this person or group. When you see what you write, you will have a good idea about what you believe to be true about this person or group and your connection to him, her or them.

Now describe in writing, in pictures or in an imagined video what change you want to see in this person or group. This is your goal. It may be specific ("hit our targets on KPIs this month") or it may be more generalized ("I want my kid to have more confidence at school.") How will you recognize that the change has happened? What behaviours, language or situations will be different after the change has happened? You are writing for yourself, but the writing is important in pushing you to really put some edges around what you want.

Your purpose is the reason you think this change would be a good thing. It's often useful to ask this question three or four times: "when the change happens, what will that get you?" Some part of what it "gets you" might be that you will be more satisfied with the state or resourcefulness of someone else. If you want your kid to be more confident, for instance, what that gets you might be that you will know she can handle herself when you're not there. When you ask the question again, you can say that if you know she can handle herself when you're not there, that might allow you to imagine that she will be able to be safe and develop in ways you haven't even imagined. When you ask again, you might get to something like the idea that you will feel happier and more satisfied because you have played a part in the development of a terrific person. And that feeling of happiness and satisfaction might get you something else. As you move up the chain, you come to something that will be a lot like a purpose, the criterion that allows you to separate what is right in your life from what needs to be made right.

Now allow yourself to sit with that purpose and notice what else comes into your awareness. Whatever other relationships, actions or memories attach themselves to this purpose, make your imagining of them vivid and compelling. See, hear, and feel them as though you had actually stepped into that situation and were fully present in it. When you are feeling that the purpose is woven through important elements in your identity and experience, write something that allows you to remember this feeling. It might be a description, a powerful word, a phrase from a song or a poem. Whatever it is, you know that when you read it again, it will bring back this powerful sense of your purpose as it relates to this particular relationship you want to influence.

Finally, imagine the first thirty seconds of the next time you see the person or group you want to influence. You might want to repeat the words or visualize an image that connects you to your purpose as you connect with this person or group. As you mentally rehearse the interaction, notice what changes when you hold steady to your purpose as you connect with this person or people. What's different now?

LIVING YOUR **PURPOSE**

Three steps to purposeful influence

1. Your goals matter. Purpose is a goal big enough to contain different actions and relationships and it is expressed as an intention to create specific results in yourself and in the world. Whether you prefer to imagine this interaction as energy or force of personality or the benefits created by strongly chosen words and actions, knowing what you want influences others in ways that are predictable even when neither you nor they are conscious of the process.

2. People are always testing. They want to know what they can trust and they want to know what they can trust in themselves. The answer to both questions is most easily found by connecting with someone who is able to hold to a purpose with congruence.

3. By comparing their search for a purpose to your congruent purpose, others will find new information about what they want. Often this takes the form of participating in your purpose while they identify how it matches or differs from their own.

DO YOU NEED A PURPOSE TO SET A GOAL?

It seems somewhat circular to argue that having a purpose is an important element in forming goals. Goals are important because they allow us to filter information about ourselves and our world, and make choices about how to pay attention and take action. Yet it is remarkably easy for clever, well-balanced people to start off in pursuit of something and then make a thousand adjustments away from that pursuit. At any given moment, their choices make sense. Cumulatively, those choices create a situation where a clever, well-balanced person no longer sees room for goals because they are so busy maintaining elements of their present life that they cannot imagine it getting better. There is no way out of this kind of bind at the level of thinking that creates it. Purpose invites a new perspective, one from which the maze of daily life can be seen and appreciated for what it gives and for what it takes to maintain it.

Purpose also challenges the notion that there is no point in making goals in unpredictable situations. As they look around their experience, many smart people realize that lots of goals are not achieved because relationships and environments are unpredictable. There is lots of science to explain that outcomes are frequently determined by conditions outside our control and even outside our awareness. If you cannot actually control whether or not you achieve something, embracing it as a goal seems risky at best, self-destructive at worst. So realistic people are often willing to settle for having values instead of goals. This is another way of saying they do the best they can given the circumstances.

Having a sense of purpose, a compelling sense of direction, creates a reason to risk setting goals and to learn from them whether or not they are achieved. A purpose is a goal so big that you do not have to find its edges for it to be useful. Part of the usefulness of a purpose is that the edges remain fuzzy enough to allow for new perceptions and defined enough to make it possible to set goals within them.

Smart people risk growth

My friend Dawn is smart. She made her way up the corporate ladder before deciding to start her own business. She loves to play with ideas and to solve puzzles and she combines that kind of analytical intelligence with a deep commitment to making things happen and a lively curiosity about how people work. In her field, she is known for managing the politics and the people so that work gets done.

The thing that you might not understand from this is that the field in which she gets paid is not the field she embraces as her purpose. Her purpose is in the field she shares with me; the one where we seek out new information about how people master themselves, their work or their circumstances. She is endlessly curious about the moment when it's possible to make a better choice and she is absolutely passionate about understanding how people who are already good at something get much better at it.

Without a sense of purpose, Dawn could play at solving puzzles and work at getting things done and generally make a very good living by figuring out how to achieve the goals that other people set. That's not enough for her. She is aware that her purpose allows her to do better work and set goals within her work, and that is still not enough. Her purpose also drives her to develop models of change, to test them in writing and programming and her own progress, and then to refine them and begin again. None of these programs has yet achieved the kind of widespread success that would allow her to make it her primary source of revenue. That doesn't matter. She keeps developing the models because the drive to master them is the central force that allows her to set goals and to set direction.

Since she identified her purpose, she has multiplied her income several times over and taken on increasingly challenging roles in her day job. Her purpose gives her a sense of autonomy even in complicated corporate situations, and allows her to navigate relationships and processes especially when the stakes are high and the pressure is on. As she sets goals that are aligned with her purpose, she makes choices for herself and the people she leads. She risks situations where goals will be hard to achieve because that is part of her purpose. She wants to find the edge of her abilities and if she occasionally steps across that edge, that is just the price of discovering where it is. She needs to know how much she has mastered so she can develop past her current limits.

Are you brave enough to ask for a miracle?

If you were given the opportunity to design exactly what you wanted, what would you change in your circumstances or yourself? What is beyond your current limits? In Solution Focused Brief Therapy, they call it the miracle question (Szabo). Say to yourself, "Imagine that a miracle happened overnight and somehow, I don't know how, the world arranged itself so that when I woke up in the morning I had what I wanted. What would I see, hear and feel that would tell me that the miracle had happened while I was asleep?" It's easier to answer when a coach or therapist is asking the question. Having someone else do the probing offers a level of safety that you do not have on your own. On your own it is hard to face the implications of your response. You do know what you want and you might be choosing not to get it. You might not get it even if you choose it.

The advantage of the miracle question is that it does not start out by asking you to articulate what you want. It begins by asking you to imagine that what you have in your life allows you to be satisfied, to live on purpose. What would need to be true in your life tomorrow for you to have this sense? There are some things that are non-negotiable. What are they for you? What must be true of yourself, your behaviour and your relationships for you to know that you are living a life well-lived? Imagine that the world arranged itself so you have all these things. What do you notice when you wake up and look around?

Of course, you might wake up and have to look hard for small differences. Perhaps you already have what you need in yourself, your relationships and your circumstances. You are doing good and doing well. Now what? Do you fine-tune or enlarge? When you imagine that you wake up and something has changed for the better, you discover that you could be doing something different, something that allows you to grow or your influence to grow. At its heart, the miracle question is a challenge. Are you willing to step up to make a miracle happen?

Three steps to aligning your goals with your purpose

1. If you know what will give meaning to this day, then you have a benchmark that allows you to filter information and activities. You know what fits and what does not fit.

2. If your activities and goals do not feel like they are in line with what you want for and from your life, then change something. You can change your goals or you can revisit your purpose. If you want to be able to more accurately predict how you will feel in response to particular achievements, you cannot compromise on this alignment. It's the measuring stick that will allow you to achieve goals and to like the results.

3. Purpose matters because it drives action. People will be influenced by the purpose that is revealed by your behaviour and trust it more than the purpose you express only in words.

The PATH to Change that Satisfies

When you know your purpose, you are ready to move forward. Sometimes your objective will be to discover more of your purpose; sometimes it will be to have a specific impact in the world; sometimes it will be to shape yourself into someone you respect. The purpose of a purpose is to drive your choices and actions. Having a purpose inevitably leads to movement. It's time to take the steps that make change happen.

Even when she was a puppy, Kylie knew that the path was the best place to walk. Kylie is my cockapoo. Half cocker spaniel and half poodle, she has always been the kind of dog that causes people to stop and coo about how cute she is. Ever since she was a puppy, she's also been quietly definite about how things should be. If we took her into a field and removed the leash, she would find the footpath beaten across the middle and walk there. We thought she would enjoy romping in the grass, but she was always on a mission. She had chosen the path as the place to move if your purpose was taking you to the other side of the field.

This is true, of course. Paths develop because one person chooses a route and other people follow in that person's footsteps because a path offers clear evidence of success in getting from A to B. After enough footsteps, the path becomes clear and then it becomes even easier to follow it to get where you want to go. Paths may not be the most obvious way for a puppy to enjoy a field, but they are good ways to move through new territory towards a common destination.

PATH also represents a process to make intentional change using the principles at the heart of NLP. You step onto the PATH when you connect with your Purpose, then you take Action that you think will move you forward, Think about the results of that action and use them to offer or ask for Help. Each step on the path is motivated or supported by the interaction of the core beliefs. If you follow this PATH, you don't have to worry about how to integrate mind and body or conscious and unconscious processes. This integration happens naturally in the steps of the path:

> Purpose: Know what you want
>
> Action: Do something to move towards what you want
>
> Thought: Evaluate the difference your action makes
>
> Help: Stabilize progress by seeking or giving help

Each step on the path requires that you ground your thoughts in the experience of your body, that you connect with resources in you and with people around you, that you recognize patterns and that you know you are going in the right direction. The five principles are embedded in the metaphor of walking along a path and noticing what helps you move with more ease, more certainty, and more satisfaction.

LIVING YOUR **PURPOSE**

The **PATH** for making things happen

Change happens all day everyday. It is harder to resist than it is to do. The PATH for making change on purpose begins with committing yourself to wanting something. Every path begins with a direction in which you will move and a destination that allows you to know that you are moving in the right direction. This destination might be a goal or a purpose. If it's a purpose, you might know it by the person you want to become, the way you want to feel, or the impact you want to have on other people.

The next stage of the PATH is action. It doesn't matter how good your purpose is if you don't take a step. It's possible your purpose is not completely formed and that the goal you are pursuing is simply the best choice that comes to mind now. If you wait for perfect understanding to match perfect conditions, then you will be waiting much too long to create more satisfaction in your life. Children don't let their lack of understanding stop them from learning. They experiment, notice their results and build understanding as they move. Entrepreneurs who wait for the perfect product or market conditions go out of business. Successful entrepreneurs would rather risk misunderstanding or mistakes than risk spending too much time and too many resources on trying to predict things that are not predictable. In all fields, satisfaction begins (and ends) with action.

Thinking comes next on the PATH and it's the kind of thought that evaluates the results of our actions. Take a step and then notice the difference. You have guessed. Now test. Ask yourself what the difference means and whether it suggests that what you are doing is in line with your purpose. If it is, you can do more of it. If it's not working, go back a step and do something else. Testing the path does not indicate a lack of either competency or trust. It does indicate that noticing progress is the best way to stay on the path and move effectively towards a purpose. The only way you know you're on the right path is to continuously test your results.

Acting then thinking is counter-intuitive. We are often told to look before we leap. What the PATH model tells us is that there are two kinds of thinking. The first is the kind that allows us to set a direction. It's creative and based in our senses and our ability to see the big picture. Although it may include lots of logic and reasoning, they are employed to reach out from what is currently real to imagine new possibilities. The more we imagine in sensory detail, the more this kind of thinking can satisfy the intention behind "look before you leap." When you build a degree of safety and realism into your purpose, your path represents firmer ground and you're more likely to move along it quickly.

The other kind of thinking is analytical and critical. This is the testing kind of thinking that is capable of noticing what we have changed with our actions and deciding whether or not that represents progress. Too much analysis and we are back to waiting for perfection before we start. Too little, and we can take many steps on a path that is going in the wrong direction. The key to good analysis is to give up knowing what we expected and find out what has actually changed. Look for the details and then build the meaning. If you start with a hypothesis you are likely to filter for the information that supports your expectations. You avoid that mistake when you clear your thoughts and simply notice difference. This is why John Grinder says that "Difference is what makes a difference" (Turtles, p. 206).

The final stage on the PATH is help. This might surprise you, but there are two great reasons to feel that your progress is not complete without giving or receiving help. The first is that human beings are brilliantly created or evolved to learn by observing other human beings. Whether or not we ask someone for help, we move most quickly towards a purpose when we look for people who are already capable of doing the things we want to do. NLP was developed primarily as a set of tools for replicating excellence. Its techniques allow people to be more effective at using the help represented by those who have walked a path before them.

We test for help when we compare our progress towards our goal before and after someone else takes an action that influences us. This influence can be direct (they intended to help us) or indirect (we observed their skill so we could replicate it). Just as our goal is not complete until it is achieved in the physical world (until we experience it in our senses), our analysis is not complete until it is confirmed by sensory experience. It is difficult to accurately observe ourselves. When we are observed by someone else or observe someone else do what we believe we are doing, we get more tangible, sensory-based information about our skills, strategies and performance. This new information will allow us to take a new action, or to consolidate the steps we have already taken.

Help also serves this function when we are the ones who do the helping. When we deliberately set out to use what we learn about our actions to help someone else, we set up a feedback loop that is much easier to monitor than the ones between ourselves and our environment. Let's take optimism as an example. There's a fair amount of research that suggests optimism improves both results and quality of life. While it may make reality look better than it is, optimism is effective in supporting useful beliefs and behaviours. But how could you tell if you were becoming more or less optimistic? Since your circumstances are changing even as you make deliberate change in your thinking and action, it's hard to self-monitor. It's much easier to see increased optimism in someone you have deliberately helped. Seeing what works for someone else is another form of testing what is likely to be working for us.

So the steps on the PATH to positive change are these: Purpose (decide what you want); Action (try something to move towards what you want); Thought (evaluate whether you are moving in the right direction) and Help (monitor and consolidate gains by observing others). Taking these steps involves five principles that describe the way people interact with other people and environments to make choices. Those principles can be represented as integration, resourcefulness, connectedness, patterns, and purpose. They describe human beings who are minds in bodies, who have what they need to be more satisfied, who progress by making connections with others and with their environment, who think and act in patterns, and who are more satisfied when they have a purpose to guide their choices. NLP does not invent these principles or steps. It is a set of tools for observing them in people who are in the process of becoming more satisfied with themselves and the results they achieve.

Could you use PATH without knowing anything about NLP? Of course you could. NLP is simply an effective coding of the natural processes for learning and leadership. The patterns identified by NLP were all being used by people before NLP was invented. The tools offered by NLP are not the only way to think about making change on purpose and the principles that drive those tools are common to many effective models of making change. NLP does provide a reliable set of tools for putting those principles to work and making the most of the PATH to living your purpose.

Next steps in NLP

Three themes run throughout this book. The first is the importance of engaging with other people so that we can learn, verify, collaborate or influence in the service of a goal or purpose. The second is that it is very hard to pull oneself into the state of relaxed detachment where resources come to the surface and new possibilities emerge. It is easier to make that change with the help of someone else. The final is that taking action is necessary, even before we are sure of all the steps. When you are ready to make more effective use of the beliefs and principles outlined in this book, you need to work with other people to prepare yourself, take action and notice what changes.

It's possible to compare and analyze this book against the reading you have done in other NLP books. That may generate interesting ideas. If you want those ideas to work for you, you must test them. The best way to evaluate any NLP book is to use it. Take an idea or exercise and try it in a real situation where you are influencing real people to move towards a real goal. Notice the results you get. If you like them, do more of what you just did. If you do not like your results, return to the book to verify your methods or read a different book.

The best way to develop further is to take a really good training. This is not as easy as it sounds. You can try asking people you know for recommendations. People will like training for different reasons. Some will report on having 'learned a lot' when what they really mean is that the presenter gave them masses of material, some of which they captured and used. Others will report on trainings being 'transformative.' Often this means that they dissociated from their problems and spent time getting in touch with resources without reintegrating them into the situations where they were in pain or stuck. They love the experience of the training, but they cannot maintain the resourcefulness when they have to step out of the sheltered environment and face their lives and problems. You will only know a good training by its testimonials when those testimonials include examples of what changed in people's lives after they took the training.

A better way to find the right training is to try some. Show up for a free introduction or ask for a meeting with a trainer. Pay for a short course. Experience the training and then go back over it and ask yourself: what is different in my life now? A good course will have planted seeds that are still growing in your thought days or weeks later. It will also have provoked you to act in ways you would not otherwise act so that you are surer that you have a purpose and that your actions are in line with it. *Guess and test.* It is the best way to get the information you need to move forward.

And as we end, my thanks for help along the way

My family is at the heart of my own life and I am grateful for the different ways they support my well-being and curiosity and work. Thank you Rob and Cary and Chris for being at the centre of my world, thank you Mom and Dad for conversations around the dinner table, and thank you to Carolina whose energy and exuberance remind me that we are all bigger on the inside than we look on the outside.

My sister, Tara Mora, is a thoughtful and motivating editor who has an incredible eye for detail. Any remaining errors are ones I added and entirely my fault.

Ron Vereggen and Andrew Freund, my training partners, have offered buckets of support and encouragement and coaching as I worked on the book and as I continue to introduce change at NLP Canada Training. Michel Neray and Roz Usheroff are professional motivators who are really, really good at cheering me on when I need it. Kathleen Milligan is my very dear friend and coach/therapist who spins the trances that keep me in touch with my resources. I am lucky to work with each of you.

Are all teachers and coaches grateful for the courage and intelligence of their clients? I am endlessly appreciative of all the students and clients of NLP Canada Training. They are curious and compassionate and brave and every one of them extends our community of practice in new and interesting ways. I have learned from every one of you. Thank you.

This book took only a few months to write after ten years of learning, practicing and developing NLP. It is appropriate to conclude with my gratitude to the founders of NLP, Richard Bandler and John Grinder. Their drive, their precise observation, and their willingness to *guess and test* provided a foundation for all that has come after. I'm also thankful that Virginia Satir and Milton Erickson allowed themselves to be observed with such relentless precision. Although I never met Milton Erickson, I am always inspired by his curiosity, his evident love of people, and his brilliance in listening, accepting, and designing interventions.

NLP is a field without a consistent body of knowledge, with some consistency in practice, and with no consistently good conversation about what works, what needs to change and what comes next. I am grateful to the authors who enrich the field with good conversation: among others, I include in this group Susie Linder Pelz and Richard Bolstad for their work relating NLP to other change models, and Andy Smith for his clear and sensible introduction to NLP. Most of what I know of NLP, I learned first from Chris Keeler, who was my trainer and then my training partner for many years. Chris shared what he learned over more than ten years of study with his NLP mentor, Derek Balmer and with John Grinder. Through Chris, I connected with the oral tradition that continues to spread many of the stories and practices of NLP.

The final person I want to thank does not yet exist, but she has lived in my heart for many years. The poet William Butler Yeats once imagined a fisherman at dawn as a representation of the kind of poetry he wanted to write. Perhaps that was at the back of my mind when this woman appeared in my thoughts, a representation of the purpose which guides me in making goals and making a difference. I am grateful for the possibility that I will one day step into her shoes.

I have in my mind a woman. She is seventy or eighty or more and she is calm and quiet and so, so strong. When I look in her eyes, I see compassion and humour and the capacity to hold many, many stories. She still has work to do. She is me. I do not remember when I met her for the first time, but she has been with me for many years. She is the frame I choose when I make choices about what is an opportunity and what is a distraction. I hold choices up to her story to discover whether they will help to bring her into being. The choices that will bring her into being are good even when they hurt or come with a high price tag. The choices that do not fit in her life story do not fit in mine. I am grateful that she is kind and patient and has already lived through all my failings. I am grateful for the twinkle in her eyes as she waits for me to catch up.

REFERENCES

Bandler, Richard and John Grinder. (1979). Frogs into Princes. Colorado: Real People Press.

Bannink, Fredrike. (2012). Practicing Positive CBT. Wiley-Blackwell.

Csikszentmihalyi, Mihaly. (2007). Flow: The Psychology of Optimal Experience. Harper Perennial.

Doidge, Norman, M.D. (2007). The Brain That Changes Itself. New York: Penguin.

Dutton, Kevin. (2011). Split-Second Persuasion: The Ancient Art and New Science of Changing Minds. Houghton-Mifflin.

Dweck, Carol S. (2006). Mindset: The New Psychology of Success. New York: Random House.

Edelman, Gerald (2005). Wider than the sky: the phenomenal gift of consciousness. Yale University Press.

Gilbert, Dan (2004). The surprising science of happiness. Retrieved from http:// www.ted.com/talks/dan_gilbert_asks_why_are_we_happy.html

Gladwell, Malcolm (1999). The physical genius. Retrieved from http://gladwell.com/the-physical-genius/

Grinder, John and Judith DeLozier (1995). Turtles All the Way Down: Prerequisites to Personal Genius. Grinder, DeLozier and Associates.

Kahneman, Daniel. Thinking Fast and Slow. New York: Doubleday.

Mau, Bruce, Jennifer Leonard, Institute Without Boundaries. (2004) Massive Change. Phaidon Press.

Pink, Dan. (2013). To Sell is Human. Riverhead Books.

Robinson, Ken. (2006). How schools kill creativity. Retrieved from http://www.ted.com/talks/ken_robinson_says_schools_kill_creativity.html

Strauss, Neil. (2005). The Game. It Books.

Szabo, Peter. nd. "An Introduction to Solution-focused Brief Coaching." Retrieved from http://www.solutionsurfers.com/pdf/IntroBriefCoaching.pdf

Yeats, W. B. (1937). A General Introduction for My Work. Retrieved from http:// www.ricorso.net/rx/library/authors/classic/Yeats_WB/prose/Essays_Intros/Gen_Introd.htm

Linda Ferguson

Linda Ferguson loves to explore the way our words shape our lives. For more than ten years, she has been a Senior Partner at NLP Canada Training. Her work there is to build a community of practice where curious people come to explore, connect, and make change happen. People come back year after year to hear new stories and refresh their curiosity about making lives better and influence stronger.

Our training brings out the smart in people. Our certifications are so engaging, surprising and practical that people find they are more capable than they thought. They walk out from training and into a vibrant world of possibility. We stay current with developments in NLP and with evidence-based practice in related fields including solution focused coaching and positive psychology. Our training is always evolving to encompass new learning and new opportunities.

Linda Ferguson holds a doctorate from the University of Toronto in English Literature. She loves the way rhythm, images and tone shape the way we talk to one another and the way talk changes us. She loves telling stories almost as much as she loves listening to them.

www.nlpcanada.com